# CORPORATE
# CANCER

# Books by Vox Day

## Nonfiction

*Jordanetics*
*SJWs Always Lie*
*SJWs Always Double Down*
*Cuckservative* (with John Red Eagle)
*On the Existence of Gods* (with Dominic Saltarelli)
*The Return of the Great Depression*
*The Irrational Atheist*

## Arts of Dark and Light

*Summa Elvetica*
*A Throne of Bones*
*A Sea of Skulls*

## Quantum Mortis

*A Man Disrupted* (with Steve Rzasa)
*Gravity Kills* (with Steve Rzasa)
*A Mind Programmed* (with Jeff and Jean Sutton)

## Eternal Warriors

*The War in Heaven*
*The World in Shadow*
*The Wrath of Angels*

## Collections

*The Altar of Hate*
*Riding the Red Horse Vol. 1* (ed. with Tom Kratman)
*There Will Be War Vol. X* (ed. with Jerry Pournelle)

# CORPORATE
# CANCER

How to Work Miracles

and Save Millions by

Curing Your Company

# VOX DAY

CASTALIA HOUSE

Corporate Cancer
How to Work Miracles and Save Millions by Curing Your Company

Vox Day

Published by Castalia House
Tampere, Finland
www.castaliahouse.com

Cover: Steve Beaulieu

ISBN: 978-952-7303-58-0

# Contents

# Introduction:
# The Death of *Star Wars*

Like many young Americans in 1977, I found myself sitting in a darkened theater, staring up at the screen in total awe as yellow words crawled towards the top. By the end of the film, I had become more than just a mere fan of *Star Wars*. I had become a bona fide fanboy. I saw it for my birthday, my best friend's birthday, my next birthday, and his next birthday too. In all, I saw it seven times before the age of ten. I regularly spent my 25-cent weekly allowance on *Star Wars* cards, managed to collect a complete blue set, and made decent headway on the red and yellow sets as well.

For Christmas, my parents gave me a *Star Wars* sweatshirt and a pair of action figures; a stormtrooper and Luke Skywalker. Over the following years, my brothers and I assembled a respectable collection; not quite sufficient to reenact the entire movie, but more than enough to stage a battle or fill a cantina.

Even as I matured into adulthood and put away the more overtly childish things, *Star Wars* remained a treasured touchstone of my childhood. I played through *Dark Forces*, *X-Wing*, and *TIE Fighter* from LucasArts, and even wrote the cover review of the latter for *Electronic Entertainment*. From time to time my friends and I would discuss how cool it would be if George Lucas ever got around to making the other two trilogies that supposedly bookended the original three movies.

And when he finally did, my best friend and I, who had first seen the movie together as children, took our wives to see *The Phantom Menace* on opening night. It was a disappointment, of course, as were the subsequent two films, and so I was pleased when Lucas decided to sell *Star Wars* to Disney for an astonishing $4 billion. After all, if there is one thing that Disney knows how to do, it is to make great movies, right? How could anything possibly go wrong?

But what I, and everyone else, including the financial analysts, neglected to account for was the fact that the Disney that acquired the rights to *Star Wars* was no longer truly the same corporation that created instant classics like *Snow White*, *The Little Mermaid*, and *The Lion King*. That Disney was long dead, and its animated corpse was now being worn like a skin suit by executives with objectives that would have been unrecognizable to Walt Disney or his successors.

Disney had been converged.

Despite the huge success of Disney's first *Star Wars* movie, *The Force Awakens*, the seeds of future failure had already been sown. Those deadly seeds began to sprout, and become recognizable, with the second film, *Rogue One*. But it wasn't until *The Last Jedi* was released that the awful truth finally became obvious to all of the real *Star Wars* fans.

Han Solo was dead. Princess Leia was (in real life) dead. Luke Skywalker was dead. And most important, the magic of a galaxy far, far away was deader than the crew of the first Death Star. *Star Wars* was dead, and it had expired on the watch of the very people who had more than 4 billion reasons to cherish, protect, and care for it. If I've just spoiled the movie for you, be thankful! I've saved you a few brain cells as well as a bit of the magic that made *Star Wars* special.

How could such a train wreck take place? How could Disney possibly permit such a thing to happen to such a valuable property?

This book is written to answer those very questions. And the answer is simple, although it will require reading further for it to be meaningful to you. *Star Wars* is dead because Disney is inflicted with the corporate cancer known as *convergence*, a lethal organizational illness that I will explain in the first chapter.

The term "convergence" is probably new to you, and I will explain it in detail, but all you need to understand for now is that convergence is *extraordinarily expensive* for the corporations that contract it. Convergence costs the average *Fortune 500* company many millions of dollars every year, and in return, produces nothing but one problem after another, each more serious than the next. And closer to home, convergence is costing *your* organization time, money, and resources that it cannot afford to lose, and it is doing so *right now*.

Consider the example of *The Last Jedi*. Despite having been a life-long fan of the series, I didn't bother seeing *The Last Jedi*. According to the box office receipts, neither did millions of former *Star Wars* fans who only two years before had propelled *The Force Awakens* to $936 million in domestic revenue, plus another $1.1 billion in foreign grosses. This was completely unexpected, given that the first two weeks of *Attack of the Clones* and *The Empire Strikes Back* had outperformed the first two weeks of Episodes 1 and 4. But in its first two weeks, the penultimate film of the nine-movie *Star Wars* saga brought in $228 million less than *The Force Awakens* had only two years before.

*The Last Jedi* bombed even worse with foreign viewers, particularly in China. In the end, the eighth episode of *Star Wars*, with its proud purple-haired Cruella De Vils, new grrrl power icons, and minority heroes, was around 35 percent, or $750 million, short of pre-release expectations. Its home video performance was even worse, as the $80 million in DVD and Blu-ray sales of *The Last Jedi* was nearly $110 million less than its predecessor. Between the lower box office, significantly reduced home video sales, and even more catastrophically shrunken merchandise sales, *The Last Jedi* underperformed by more than $1 billion dollars thanks to the movie's convergence.

But the greatest cost of the convergence of *Star Wars* was to its brand. The box office failure of *Solo: A Star Wars Story*, which has been widely derided by former *Star Wars* fans as *Soylo* for the way in which the roguish space smuggler was reinvented as a soyboy more palatable to social justice tastes, strongly suggests that the *Star Wars* brand has lost its magic. The idea that a *Star Wars* movie would be trounced at the box office by a minor superhero sequel would have been unthinkable only four years ago, and yet *Solo* only brought in $375 million compared to $721 million for *Deadpool 2*.

As if that wasn't bad enough, the final film in the nonology, *Episode IX: The Rise of Skywalker*, is projected to open at less than three-quarters of the Episode VII opening weekend, and at $550 million, is expected to bring in only 58.6 percent of *The Force Awakens*'s domestic box office. And while the third movie in a *Star Wars* trilogy customarily doesn't do as well as the first one, the difference between this estimate and the track record of the two previous trilogies indicates that between the domestic box office, the international box office, and the home market, the corporate cancer of social justice convergence will cost Disney close to $2 BILLION on the final trilogy alone.

The costs of corporate cancer can be expensive indeed, and these costs are not limited to Hollywood. As you will see again and again, convergence consistently drives customers away, reduces revenue, destroys brands, and chases away anticipated sales. And yet, convergence is a cancer that corporations often *voluntarily contract* in the name of diversity, equality, gender-neutrality, inclusivity, progress, the current year, or some other aspect of social justice.

Social justice convergence is a corporate cancer that can be fatal, but fortunately, it is a disease that is both curable and avoidable. The purpose of this book is to transform you into a corporate surgeon who possesses both the knowledge and the expertise to remove it from your organization, benefit from its absence, and prevent its reoccurrence.

# Chapter I

## Convergence

*Society should treat all equally well who have deserved equally well of it, that is, who have deserved equally well absolutely. This is the highest abstract standard of social and distributive justice; towards which all institutions, and the efforts of all virtuous citizens should be made in the utmost degree to converge.*

—John Stuart Mill, *Utilitarianism*

In 1861, the English philosopher John Stuart Mill published his most important work, *Utilitarianism*. In it, he imagined a new form of justice, one that involved society as a whole instead of the various individual forms that had previously defined the concept.

Although utilitarianism was eventually rejected by philosophers as a failed attempt at moral democracy, this new definition of justice by Mill somehow survived his philosophy's demise. Without ever being specifically endorsed by any intellectual figure or movement of note, social justice gradually evolved into an alternative to traditional morality and traditional measures of correct behavior.

Those who believed in social justice entered academia in the latter half of the 20th century and gradually gained influence in the university system over a period of decades. Now, social justice has become the primary philosophy espoused by university administrators and academics alike. The American university has become a secular church of social justice, providing an ever-evolving moral standard that serves as a substitute for both the public rule of law and private morality. University students are indoctrinated in social justice philosophy, which in a nutshell amounts to competitive martyrdom. After graduation, they either go to graduate school or go forth into the corporate world to spread the gospel of social justice.

The social justice gospel comes in a variety of forms, which include tolerance, equality, progress, inclusivity, and diversity. It condemns a considerable collection of secular sins, which range from microaggressions and unconscious bias to institutional racism, institutional sexism, and institutional cis-sexuality. Social justice abolishes the historic concepts of normalcy and meritocracy in the name of the different and the disadvantaged.

Now, it is very important to understand that for the purposes of this book, *it does not matter in the slightest* whether the advocates of social justice are right to believe what they do or not. It is irrelevant if they are right to engage in public witch hunts to disemploy corporate crimethinkers or if they are wrong to do so. It makes *no difference whatsoever* if they are the next stage in human moral evolution or a maleducated, overmedicated mob of supremely sensitive snowflakes.

We are officially agnostic on the subject.

I won't pretend that I don't have a personal opinion on the matter. But my opinion doesn't matter when it comes to the consequences. And, by the way, your opinion doesn't matter either. In the same way that it doesn't matter if we happen to believe that gravity is good or evil when it comes to determining how fast we fall, in the corporate context, it doesn't matter if we think social justice is a great leap forward for humanity, a necessary evil to be endured, or an insane monstrosity that should be killed with fire.

All that concerns us is whether or not there are observable actions that reliably lead to predictable consequences.

In most cases, the only gravity-related measure that is relevant to the analysis is how hard the object in question is going to hit the ground.

As far as this book goes, the only social justice-related measure that is relevant is whether social justice is good for your business or if it is bad for your business. And, as you will see, as it is *very* easy to demonstrate, social justice is bad for business. It is *very bad* for business. In fact, it is so bad for business that the more completely devoted the corporation is to social justice, the less able it is able to perform its primary function.

Convergence describes the degree to which an organization prioritizes social justice. There are five stages of convergence:

1. **Infiltrated.** The corporation has been entered by people devoted to social justice, but they do not have any significant influence or authority within the company. Employees are hired, fired, and promoted on the basis of either merit or connections. The marketing tends to reflect the company's products and services.

2. **Lightly Converged.** The social justice infiltrators have begun to move into their preferred areas, such as Human Resources and Marketing, but they don't have any real influence over the corporation's policies or corporate strategies. The company starts to make occasional noises about "outreach" and "diversity", but doesn't actually change its employment practices. The marketing is still mostly about the company's products, but increasingly features improbably diverse scenarios.

3. **Moderately Converged.** Social justice advocates now control Human Resources, which is used as a corporate high ground to exert influence over other departments as well as the executive team. The corporate marketing begins to devote more attention to signaling corporate virtue than selling its products. Managers are encouraged to hire diverse candidates and pressured to stop holding low-performance employees accountable. HR begins holding mandatory awareness sessions and hiring diversity consultants. The corporation's customer service begins to go downhill.

4. **Heavily Converged.** Social justice advocates now control the corporate high ground and the strategic centers. Significant elements of the executive team and the board are devoted to social justice, often in a very public manner. Implicit hiring quotas are imposed and it becomes almost impossible to fire anyone for anything short of murder in the workplace. HR openly dictates corporate policy to employees, often without consulting the executives. The marketing materials not only signal corporate virtue, but openly advocate various social justice issues. The corporation shows indifference to its core customer base and begins to focus obsessively on new markets that mostly exist in its imagination.

5. **Fully Converged.** The corporation devotes significant resources to social causes that have absolutely nothing to do with its core business activities. Human Resources is transformed into a full Inquisition, imposing its policies without restraint and striking fear into everyone from the Chairman of the Board on down. The CEO regularly mouths social justice platitudes in the place of corporate strategies, and the marketing materials are so full of virtue-signaling and social justice advocacy that it becomes difficult to tell from them what the company actually does or sells. The corporation now shows open contempt for its customers.

These five stages of convergence can be usefully compared to the five stages of cancer, both in terms of the way in which cancer spreads throughout the human body and the increased risk to the patient's life that correlates with the spread of the cancer.

- **Stage 0**: is a group of abnormal cells known as *carcinoma in situ*. There is some disagreement in the medical community about whether this stage should actually be considered cancer or not. Either way, the prognosis for those diagnosed with breast cancer discovered at this stage is very good, with a five-year survival rate of 93 percent.

- **Stage I**: cancers are localized to one part of the body. Stage I cancer can be surgically removed if small enough. The five-year survival rate for breast cancer is still high, at 88 percent.
- **Stage II**: cancers are locally advanced. Stage II cancer can be treated by chemo, radiation, or surgery. The five-year survival rate is 78 percent.
- **Stage III**: cancers are further locally advanced. Whether a cancer is designated as Stage II or Stage III can depend on the specific type of cancer. Stage III can be treated by chemo, radiation, or surgery. The five-year survival rate is 52 percent.
- **Stage IV**: cancers have often metastasized, or spread to other organs or throughout the body. Stage IV cancer can be treated by chemo, radiation, or surgery. The five-year survival rate is 15 percent.

Most cancer patients suffering from advanced Stage IV cancers do not live very long. However, a corporation that is completely converged can survive almost indefinitely as long as it can find funding to replace its previous sources of revenue. But even if a completely converged corporation remains technically "alive", it is no longer functional and it is totally unable to perform its previous reason for existence any longer.

Imagine, for example, the case of a professional basketball team that is so completely converged that it abandons the traditional principle of sporting meritocracy, and due to its commitment to equality, decides to field a team comprised of players equally distributed by sex, race, height, and weight. Even though the team proceeds to lose all its games and all of its fans stop attending the games by the time the season ends, the team does not go out of business. Instead, the team continues to pay the salaries of its executives and its employees, and it will continue to do so as long as it keeps receiving its share of television revenue from the league.

And when the basketball league's commissioner kicks the converged team out of the league the next season and it no longer receives any television revenue, it still manages to survive, in a manner of speaking. It does so by finding both a) corporations run by equality-minded executives willing to sponsor the team, and, b) government agencies able to provide government funding to support its commitment to equality. In fact, the converged basketball team might hope to become even more profitable than when it was a real team that played actual basketball games, because it no longer has any need to pay its players or play any games. The team still survives, in a corporate sense, and its executives are still taking home their fat salaries, but the team is no longer able to play basketball games or entertain basketball fans.

Which tends to raise an obvious philosophical question: can a fully-converged basketball team still be considered a basketball team any more?

Come to think of it, I suspect I may have just explained the hitherto inexplicable existence of the WNBA! But that will have to be fully investigated in another book.

This scenario of a non-basketball-playing basketball team may sound crazy to you. It may sound impossible. But then, look at the behavior of some of the organizations around you, from the National Football League to Marvel Comics.

It is definitely crazy, but it is very, very far from impossible.

# Chapter 2

## The Costs of Convergence: Top Line

It's one thing to simply claim that something is bad, it is another to demonstrate exactly how bad it is. Once a corporation contracts Stage Five convergence, it can go downhill very fast.

How fast? On average, as a rough estimate, up to 20 percent *in just one year*.

This decline can take place in terms of either revenue or units.

Usually, the decline takes place in terms of the metric that is more important. For example, converged companies that suffer falling unit sales will often attempt to conceal their collapsing revenues by raising their prices. The comics industry did this when it raised its average price per comic from $3.13 to $3.99 over the last decade. Such a measure only increases the speed of the subsequent decline, as the Law of Supply and Demand suggests, but it often succeeds in fooling casual observers into thinking the company or industry is healthier than it actually is.

This concealment of decreasing demand for its products is one reason why, when big, previously successful businesses collapse, they tend to collapse very quickly. Once the snowball starts rolling down the hill, it is very hard to stop it.

The unexpected decline in box office revenue for *Star Wars Episode VIII: The Last Jedi* mentioned in the introduction is an excellent example of the negative effect that convergence has on a corporation's top line. Another example of convergence striking an organization that is at the very height of its success and popularity is the National Football League and its response to the anti-police protests by some of its players.

San Francisco 49ers quarterback Colin Kaepernick began sitting during the pre-game national anthem during a preseason game before the 2016 season. It took three weeks for anyone to notice, but once they did, it was readily apparent that NFL fans were displeased by the league's uncharacteristic failure to fine Kaepernick or any of the players who joined his protest by kneeling while the anthem was played. This permissiveness was astonishing from a league that has been known to fine players as much as $20,000 for crimes such as wearing shoes that are the wrong color, a baseball cap with a cross on it, and socks that are too low.

The league's failure to act was correctly interpreted by fans as a very public endorsement of social justice by a league office that has been increasingly prone to virtue-signaling in recent years. One reliable sign of corporate convergence is a stubborn refusal to listen to very clear messages being sent by the corporation's customer base. Convergence exchanges the traditional business principle that the customer is always right for the social justice principle that the unhappy customer is always racist, sexist, and outdated, which means his complaints should be ignored.

In the case of the NFL, the fans complaints were not only ignored, they were actively denied by league officials, including the NFL Commissioner. A variety of alternative explanations were offered, from interest in the U.S. Presidential election to sub-par officiating, until the continuing decline had gone on too long and become too large to credibly explain away.

Throughout the 2017 season, more and more NFL fans simply turned off their televisions and stopped attending games, as television audiences shrank by as much as 41 percent and social media was filled with images of half-empty stadiums. The total revenue loss to the league from television alone is expected to be in excess of $500 million, and while the attendance problem did not significantly affect 2017 revenues—tickets to NFL games are mostly presold—the material impact of the decline was felt in 2018.

While the NFL continues to publicly dismiss its declining ratings as a temporary problem, the fact is that they caused the league to fall short of its predicted 2017 revenue of $14 billion and knocked the league considerably off the track of its revenue target of $25 billion by 2027. A four-percent reduction in annual revenue may not sound like much, but it represents a 10.7 percent decline in expected revenues which is not insignificant to any business, no matter how big it is. Indeed, there are even some who believe that this unnecessary, convergence-caused debacle may represent Peak NFL.

The NFL's woes continued unabated into the 2019 season. The damage done to the NFL's brand wasn't a temporary hiccup in performance. They've turned away hardcore, long-term fans from the game. This is most readily demonstrated not by ratings, but by the empty seats that abound at games. After all, who are your hardest-core fans of all? The suburbanites sitting on their recliners, or the crazies in facepaint wearing your team's expensive jerseys and slurping $10 beers in the stands? Many of those fans have still not returned to NFL games. While TV broadcasts carefully film the games to avoid televising large numbers of empty seats, fans constantly post pictures and videos of sparsely populated stadiums—most often mistakenly placing the blame on their fellow fans instead of the teams that have driven them away. These social media posts are gleefully collected by Breitbart News and other conservative media sites with headlines like "Weak Four: NFL Still Hasn't Found the Answer for Empty Seats".

But the convergence of the NFL did not begin with the anthem protests. It began with Pinktober and *fútbol americano* and the Rooney Rule. Although total NFL revenue did not peak until 2016, its television ratings actually maxed out the year before. At the end of the 2017 season, average viewership per game had fallen to 14.9 million, down 9.7 percent for the year and 16.8 percent since it peaked at 17.9 million per game in 2015.

With 256 games per season, that two-year decline in viewership represents 768 million lost game-viewings. Convergence is *costly*.

Only time will tell, but if the history of converged corporations is a reliable guide, the future is much more likely to witness annual NFL revenues falling below $10 billion than to see them exceed the $25 billion projected by Commissioner Goodell, barring any Zimbabwe-style inflation blowing up the U.S. economy in dollar terms.

Marvel Comics may provide an informative trajectory for the possible future of an increasingly converged NFL. In 2007, Marvel took in 45 percent of the revenue from a comics market that sold 85 million units. It seemingly went from strength to strength, as it released its first *Iron Man* movie the next year, which brought in $585 million at the box office. In 2009, the company that had filed for bankruptcy in 1996 was bought for $4 billion by Disney.

This was an astonishing turnaround by a failing organization, a true business success story, and many analysts expected Marvel to continue to build upon its success. But again, the one thing that they did not count upon was the fact that Marvel had been entirely converged, and what's more, the security of being owned by Disney permitted Marvel executives to let their social justice freak flag fly.

It would be hard to find a social justice cause that Marvel did not enthusiastically endorse in recent years. From gay weddings and interracial relationships to female obesity, short hair, and girl power, Marvel *relentlessly* preached tolerance, equality, progress, inclusivity, and diversity to its comics buyers, even going so far as to replace Tony Stark with a black girl genius, Thor with a woman, Peter Parker with both a half-black Hispanic and a woman, Bruce Banner with a Korean-American genius, Wolverine with his cloned daughter, and Carol Danvers with a Muslim girl.

Marvel also introduced new characters, such as America Chavez, billed excitedly as "the first Latin-American LGBTQ character to star in their own series."

When Marvel met with criticism after introducing *Spider-Man* replacement Miles Morales, aka Kid Arachnid, in 2011, Marvel's editor-in-chief Axel Alonso responded "Simple fact is Marvel Comics reflect the world in all its shapes, sizes and colors. We believe there's an audience of people out there who is thirsty for a character like Miles Morales." Original *Spider-Man* creator Stan Lee supported Alonso, saying, "Doing our bit to try to make our nation, and the world, color blind is definitely the right thing."

But whether doing their bit to impose color blindness on world is right or not, their belief in the *size* of that audience was evidently misguided. Six years later, Alonso is out of a job, the most recent *Spider-Man* issue featuring Peter Parker has sold nearly a million units, while the Miles Morales version has seen one series after another shut down after only 12 issues.

*After one year, Brian Michael Bendis' new comic chronicling the further of adventures of Miles Morales has lost almost two-thirds of its readership.*

—"Spider-Man Comics Sales Estimates for February 2017",
Mike McNulty

Just to add insult to injury, *Spider-Woman Vol. 6* was canceled after only 17 issues, due to a 77 percent decline from its initial monthly sales of 53,885. Marvel's editorial staff, largely young white women, seem unconcerned by the sales trend. They're too busy posting selfies of their weekly milkshake group to social media.

As a result of its convergence, despite a ten-year string of successful movies and television shows that constantly advertise its famous characters to the public, Marvel has been replaced as the industry's market leader by DC Comics and now only captures 38 percent of the revenue from a 74-million-unit-selling market. None of the top seven-selling comics, and only two of the top ten, are now published by Marvel. Due to its convergence, Marvel takes in a smaller piece of a smaller pie despite the many advantages it enjoys being a wholly-owned subsidiary of a hugely powerful conglomerate.

If we compare Marvel's present position in the comics market to the one it held ten years ago, the annual cost of convergence to Marvel has been around $12 million, or 21.4 percent of its current revenue. And this annual cost does not include the opportunity costs or the potential sales growth that were thrown away by Marvel's refusal to focus on what its customers wanted rather than its social justice values.

And the costs of convergence in the market leader have affected the entire industry. The convergence-related decline in the comics industry's sales that was observed in 2017, in which unit sales dropped 10.1 percent and 2.5 percent of the retail outlets went out of business, has continued in 2018. As of May, unit sales had fallen another 9.7 percent, on track to sell fewer copies than the previous annual low of 2001. Although most comic fans decry the loss of the local comic shop as an institution, the sad state of the industry is such that many local shops have been converged on a much smaller scale.

Marvel's downward trajectory is why we can reasonably conclude that if the NFL refuses to change its ways, instead of growing its revenue to $25 billion by 2027, its increasing commitment to social justice causes will eventually cause the leading sports league's annual revenues to fall to around $10 billion. With up to $1.5 billion coming off the projected top line every year, social justice convergence can only be described as an incredibly expensive indulgence for a corporation.

The fall of NASCAR, which as recently as 2005 was believed to be in a position to challenge the NFL as the most popular spectator sport in the United States, is also extremely educational in this regard. An article in *Fortune* glowingly described NASCAR as "the fastest-growing, best-run sports business in America" and quoted a marketing firm that rated NASCAR as the second-most-valuable corporate brand in the world.

*TV ratings are soaring. Corporate money is flowing. And the crowds just keep getting bigger. How NASCAR is racing ahead.*

—"America's Fastest Growing Sport", *Fortune*,
September 5, 2005

Like Marvel and the NFL, NASCAR's executives decided that the best way to continue their success and grow their rapidly expanding market was to embrace social justice while disregarding the preferences of its longtime, die-hard supporters.

NASCAR had already created its Diversity Internship Program to diversify and enrich its fan and employee bases across the motorsports industry in order to help "students from diverse backgrounds to professional opportunities in NASCAR" six years before. In 2004 NASCAR launched its Drive for Diversity Driver Development Program, "the sport's foremost attempt at integrating minority and female drivers into a predominantly white, predominantly male realm."

And in 2010, to much acclaim by the media, Danica Patrick was signed by top NASCAR team JR Motorsports and began her high-profile NASCAR career sponsored by GoDaddy.com.

NASCAR President Mike Helton had already made it clear that the motorsport league's nods to social justice were more than just gestures; they had become a fundamental part of NASCAR's conscious decision to reject its Southern white male past in favor of its diverse new future. In the lead-up to the 2006 Daytona 500, Helton said, "We believe strongly that the old, Southeastern redneck heritage that we had is no longer in existence. But we also realize that there's going to have to be an effort on our part to convince others to understand that."

Those old Southeastern redneck fans promptly responded to NASCAR's very public commitment to convergence by turning off their televisions and failing to show up at the track. The 2006 Daytona 500 was watched by nearly 20 million viewers. Ten years later, only 11.4 million people watched the 2016 Daytona 500.

The tremendous collapse in spectator interest was reflected throughout NASCAR as television viewership for NASCAR races fell from 9 million viewers per race in 2005 to 4.6 million in 2016, while track attendance revenue dropped from its 2007 peak of $430 million to only $240 million in 2015.

Despite its annual losses of $21.1 million in racetrack revenue and 400,000 television viewers per race, plus another $50 million per year from an expired sponsorship contract that Sprint declined to renew in 2015, NASCAR remains undeterred in its commitment to social justice. In November 2017, the creator of NASCAR's Drive for Diversity program, Max Siegel, looked back on his creation with satisfaction as the 2018 Drive for Diversity Development Team was announced.

*This has really been a joint effort and a true collaboration and partnership. When I think back to 10 years ago, it really makes me feel good about where we are today.*

It is obvious that whatever Mr. Siegel's metric for success might have been, NASCAR revenue and television ratings were not two of them.

Converged companies always double down on social justice. They simply can't conceive of moderating their position to appeal to a broad spectrum of fans, as normal organizations do. NASCAR has pushed even further in what sane onlookers would be forgiven for believing is an attempt to drive *all* of their remaining fans away from their races.

The latest move by NASCAR is to go after the gun culture embraced by their fandom by curtailing ads from gun makers. K-VAR, the largest supplier of firearms and accessories online, was one of 17 retailers and manufacturers of firearms and related products that signed up to advertise during NASCAR's 2019 season. Months after buying advertisement slots, K-VAR was contacted by the advertising sales agent who put the deal together with bad news: NASCAR was no longer interested in accepting K-VAR's advertising money.

The sales agent told K-VAR, "We just heard from NASCAR on a number of gun-related ads and unfortunately, due to a gradual shift in NASCAR's position on guns, these ads must be edited/changed—especially those that are depicted as assault-style rifles/sniper rifles. NASCAR is still open to some of the less controversial gun accessories, concealed carry, or classes."

What company on earth, knowing its primary consumer base is strongly attached to God, guns, and Old Glory, would turn away gun advertising? What company facing steeply falling revenues would actively turn away a significant advertising contract? The answer is a company that has either completely lost touch with its traditional customers or become completely disinterested in retaining them. In other words, a converged company.

NASCAR probably thinks in part that it can successfully shift advertising and support to whatever causes it wants, mistakenly believing NASCAR nation will follow it to whatever cause it chooses to push. This assumption is based in part on the brand's successful shift away from tobacco, which was the primary sponsor of NASCAR for decades. But this is a critical miscalculation by NASCAR for several reasons.

First, Big Tobacco was not considered to be a political issue. The vast majority of Americans, including its fan base, were already beginning to turn away from tobacco, which was once heavily promoted at NASCAR races and on many pieces of team merchandise. Society shifted away from tobacco, and NASCAR simply made that shift in time with its fans. Second, the NASCAR shift away from tobacco occurred just before multiple levels of government passed laws against tobacco sponsorship and promotion of sporting events. If any NASCAR fans were truly upset by their favorite race changing sponsors, the organization could blame the government, a tried-and-true excuse especially compelling for NASCAR's conservative-leaning core audience of Southrons.

What's next for NASCAR? Perhaps an environmentalist push that replaces its powerful engineering marvels with smart cars or electric scooters. Does that seem far-fetched? You're still underestimating the self-destructive power of corporate convergence!

The powerful commitment to social justice demonstrated by NASCAR, Marvel Comics, and the NFL may well be considered admirable by those who share social justice values. But regardless of what you think of social justice, it cannot be denied that convergence has a powerfully negative effect on a corporation's gross income, its customer base, and its brand.

And the astute observer will note that convergence can cost a corporation between five and 20 percent of its annual revenue for more than a decade *without the corporation even admitting that it has a problem*, much less doing anything to address it.

# Chapter 3

## The Costs of Convergence: Bottom Line

The cost of lost customers and prospective sales are not the only ones that convergence imposes on a corporation. Although they are more visible, those top line costs only tend to appear once the corporation has reached Stage Four convergence, and they may not be clearly visible until Stage Five convergence is achieved.

And by then, it is much too late to do anything about it.

Fortunately, there are also a number of costs that are internal to the corporation which appear much earlier in the convergence process. While they are not as apparent to the untrained eye, you can quickly learn to spot these early signs of a growing problem and shut the process down before the convergence spreads any further.

There are two departments where convergence first develops inside the average corporation:

- Human Resources (HR)
- Marketing

Of the two, Human Resources is by far the most dangerous. This is because it is the main point of entry into the corporation and it serves as an easily-controlled choke point for employees whose values and objectives are not in line with those of the corporation's executives and shareholders. For example, social justice warriors in HR use execrable Codes of Conduct to drive out stubborn white males who insist on working in a meritocracy instead of a social justice collective.

Human Resources is a more significant contributor to corporate costs than most executives realize. It is collectively a $400 billion annual industry, of which approximately half is spent on HR salaries, 42 percent is spent on external services, content, and contractors, and the remaining 8 percent goes to HR tools and technology.

On the salary side, there are 1.4 HR department staff members for every 100 workers in corporate America, and these employees are slightly more expensive than the average employee, as they account for 1.6 percent of the average corporation's total operating cost. These costs are particularly expensive for smaller companies, as those with less than 250 employees spend, on average, $2,375 per employee on their HR function.

That may not sound like much, except that the biggest and most successful companies in the world, the *Fortune 500*, only average $31,560 in profit per employee. In smaller companies, the cost of Human Resources can easily exceed half of its net profit per employee.

But isn't HR necessary? Even if it doesn't produce any corporate income directly itself, doesn't it act as a vital force multiplier that more than justifies its costs by improving the quality and productivity of the employees who actually produce revenue? Well, according to the human resources specialists themselves, HR does materially improve the quality of the employee base. As to whether that amount of improvement is justified by the expense, that is, to put it mildly, *questionable*.

We are reliably informed by a human resources expert that "the data shows a huge disparity between well run and poorly run HR teams" and that HR teams can be divided into four kinds: Level 1 (compliance driven), Level 2 (fundamental), Level 3 (Strategic), and Level 4 (Business-Integrated). Level 4 is deemed to be the most effective, as per the Human Resources Maturity Model:

- **Level 1: Compliance-Driven HR Services.** No HR strategy. "Personnel" function mostly separate from the business and talent needs. Line managers perform HR activities as they see best.
- **Level 2: Fundamental HR Services.** HR strategy partially or fully defined. Siloed HR functions. Some standardized processes and policies and core services managed well. Some automated talent systems but little integration of data.
- **Level 3: Strategic HR Department.** HR strategy aligned with business strategy. HR business supports business needs. Initiatives split between HR process improvements and talent needs. Some system integration.
- **Level 4: Business-Integrated HR.** HR strategy part of the business strategy. HR helps to drive business decisions through people, data and insights. Business and HR systems integrated and advanced.

*Level 4 companies spend almost twice per employee on HR than Level 1 companies ($4,434 vs. $2,112 per employee) and they are getting much better business outcomes. Their voluntary turnover rates, for example, are 30% lower than those at Level 1 (8% vs. 11%). This is a striking difference: these Level 4 companies are investing much more heavily in management training, employee development, coaching, productivity programs, and programs to promote wellness and work-life balance. The result is happier employees, lower turnover, and a much stronger employment brand.*

—Josh Bersin, founder and principal at Bersin by Deloitte, leading provider of research-based membership programs in human resources (HR), talent and learning

Keeping in mind that $4,434 per employee represents 14 percent of the net profit for the most successful corporations in the world, and may exceed the total profit per employee of a typical small or medium-sized business, is that really worth a three-point reduction in annual employee turnover?

In fact, wouldn't simply paying an additional $4,434 to each employee as an annual bonus likely reduce your company's voluntary turnover rate even more? It wouldn't surprise me if even a $3k bonus would reduce turnover by an astonishing 50 percent!

Of course, there are other benefits provided by these expensive Business-Integrated HR departments. Such as, we are told, integrating the HR strategy with the business strategy and helping to drive business decisions through people, data, and insights.

But what does that actually mean?

Translating from corporate consultant-speak, Business-Integrated Human Resources means letting HR run the business according to its objectives and values rather than those of the rest of the corporation, including the executives and shareholders. As you can see, this is a model that can be effectively used to sell structured convergence to any executive foolish enough to buy into the concept and pay for it.

And we have already seen from the examples of *Star Wars*, Marvel, NASCAR, and the NFL how those objectives tend to depart greatly from the traditional business objectives of providing quality products and services, building a loyal customer base, increasing brand and shareholder value, growing sales and maximizing profit.

It is true that every business beyond a certain size needs someone to do the hiring and firing, handle the payroll, and ensure that the business is in compliance with the relevant legal regulations. And it does have a legitimate employee-policing role in order to ensure that the company won't be sued for various forms of intra-corporate employee misbehavior. But just as no corporation sets up a Business-Integrated Janitorial Department or concerns itself with whether its janitorial strategy is fully integrated with its business strategy, no smart corporate executive or manager will ever hand over his decision-making responsibilities to an ever-rapacious HR department, no matter how helpful they promise to be.

## Marketing

In the United Kingdom, Christmas is marked every year by the release of the big Christmas commercials by the elite retail chains. These famous television commercials from Marks & Spencer, John Lewis, and Sainsbury's are much-anticipated events, as they are famous for being expensive, well-produced miniature films that often become cultural touchstones. Sometimes they are funny, but more often they are sentimental heart warmers designed to summon a nostalgic tear that will trickle down over the stiffest British upper lip.

Convergence strikes again.

John Lewis is the king of the Christmas commercial. Its famous 2010 Red Dress advert featured the life of one woman from birth to old age as she goes through all of the stages of life while wearing a red dress. It's a touching little piece, a brilliant advertisement that is well worth seeing, and it boosted Christmas sales at John Lewis by 39.7 percent that year.

The 2017 ad, which featured an oversized Muppet called Moz and a little mixed-race boy was equally well-received, but only by the marketing experts. They were particularly excited by the diversity and the interracial aspects of the ad.

*Hurray for seeing some diversity on such an epic advertising moment—my surprise at the mixed-race parents shows how rarely we see it in the advertising world.*

—Zoe Harris, group marketing director and head of invention, *Trinity Mirror*

How rarely indeed! However, the 2017 Christmas season was marked by an unusual series of identical rarities. It wasn't merely John Lewis, but also Marks & Spencer, Debenhams and Sainsbury's, who each independently decided to feature mixed-race couples celebrating

Christmas together in their big holiday advertisement. Even more remarkably, *every single one of them* just happened to feature a black man with a white woman, which, given the present UK demographics, can only be described as extraordinarily improbable.

After all, there are more Indians, Pakistanis, Chinese, and other Asians in the UK than there are blacks. Where were they?

Unlike the USA, the United Kingdom tracks ethnicity rather closely, so we can accurately determine exactly how statistically improbable these expensive Christmas advertisements were. As it turns out, there is only a one-in-327 chance that such a couple would be randomly selected. And the chance of all five commercials just happening to feature that particular pairing is one in 3,738,856,210,407.

That is one in 3.7 trillion, more or less. So, it wasn't just a series of coincidences. It was evidence of convergence in the British advertising industry.

You will probably not be surprised to learn that these converged commercials did not prove to be very popular with the British public over the 2017 Christmas season. As a result, John Lewis was forced to cut its prices to prevent its year-on-year sales from falling and stated that its holiday sales "will negatively affect full-year financial results". Marks & Spencer saw its clothing and home sales fall 3 percent, while Debenhams warned that its profits would be about 30% lower than expected and now faces layoffs and store closures.

> *Debenhams is to cut jobs and consider more store closures after a poor festive trading period led to a major profits warning.*
>
> > —"Debenhams job cuts and store closures likely after disappointing sales", *The Guardian*, January 18, 2018

Once might be bad luck. Twice might be an honest mistake. Five times is convergence.

Now, whether you believe interracial pairings are an abomination before God or an inspiring step towards a new era of human peace, equality, and understanding is totally irrelevant. The point is that spending £7 million on an advertisement that is guaranteed to alienate *even a very small* percentage of your customer base is an extraordinarily foolish, self-destructive act for any corporation.

Of course, it is as difficult to quantify the costs of converged marketing as it is to measure the benefits of effective marketing. But it is important to understand that just like these elite, well-funded marketing departments, your marketing department may be more interested in pushing its own values and objectives than in performing its core function of helping your company sell its products and services.

The situation is much the same in the United States. A simple image search for "white married couple" on Google doesn't provide the sort of results you would tend to expect. Of the first 25 couples shown, only 14 were actually white. The rest were either interracial or black, including one Asian male-Black female couple that is one of the statistically most unlikely marital pairings on the planet.

This is convergence. Nor should it be a surprise, as Google is one of the most completely converged corporations on the planet, because its present duopoly with Facebook in the digital advertising market means that it can afford to be stupid.

The primary takeaway here is that if your marketing department is attempting to sell *anything* that is not directly related to your core products and services, then its entire budget is a cost that is wasted, most likely on one social justice objective or another. In that case, you would be wise to follow the example of Restoration Hardware's CEO, who canceled the entire budget for his online marketing team after he learned that despite the 3,200 keywords the team had purchased, 98 percent of the company's site traffic was still coming from just 22 keywords—Restoration Hardware, and the top 21 ways to incorrectly spell it.

How much marketing money is your company wasting? The average company spends 11 percent of its total budget on marketing, which does not necessarily include the expense of the people employed in the marketing department. However, marketing only drives revenue growth at 38 percent of companies with marketing departments, which should not be a surprise when you consider how converged marketing departments so frequently produce advertising designed to lecture, shame, and even offend the company's customers.

So take a very close look at what sort of materials are being created by your marketing department. See if they are intended to actually sell your company's products or if they are intended for some other purpose. Given the level of convergence in the average marketing department, there is a very good chance that you could slash your total corporate budget by 10 percent or more and actually see your sales *rise* as a consequence of refraining from attacking your core customer base.

## Diversity and Training

While the costs of corporate convergence are usually somewhat concealed from the casual observer, there is one aspect of those costs that are open and undeniable. Increasingly, social justice advocates are carving out their own space within corporations by creating diversity departments that are spun off from Human Resources and provided their own independent budgets.

At present, these diversity departments are very small. At *Fortune 1000* companies, they have budgets that average around $1.5 million per year. However, these new developments indicate a rapid rate of increase in the costs required for diversity, because in corporations where the responsibility for overseeing diversity is under the control of the Human Resources department, the average annual diversity budget is less than one-fifth the size, at $239,000.

The bright future of well-funded diversity departments and their growing cost to corporate budgets can be anticipated by looking at what some of the most converged corporations in the United States are doing. In 2015, Intel announced a $300 million commitment to diversity, pledging to spend $60 million per year by 2020 in order to establish a $300 million fund to be used by 2020 to improve the diversity of the company's work force.

This expensive program was supplemented by Intel Capital's Diversity Initiative, which at $125 million, is "the largest venture capital resource ever created to focus on underrepresented entrepreneurs."

Although these costs are relatively small, the primary problem with diversity departments is that they represent a one-hundred percent pure waste of corporate resources. They simply do not deliver even the most basic results that one might expect from them.

For example, Bank of America possesses an award-winning diversity program that includes executive and regional inclusion councils, affinity groups, and diversity networks. All of this expensive diversity outreach did not prevent the bank from being hit with multiple racial discrimination lawsuits, including one $60 million claim by a former Bank of America employee, and another claim involving a BoA subsidiary that required multiple trials taking place over 24 years before it was finally settled for just $1 million.

There is no point in paying protection money that does not provide protection.

However, the real cost to the bottom line imposed by corporate convergence is the effect that it has on employee productivity through four factors:

- reducing the amount of time spent actually working by requiring attendance at training and meetings not directly related to work functions;
- hiring less productive, less skilled employees from the favored identity groups;
- reducing the efficiency of the employees from the more productive, more skilled identity groups; and
- introducing inefficiency through diversity-related friction.

These costs are difficult to quantify precisely, as fewer than five percent of the companies with diversity programs even attempt to calculate any sort of return on investment for them, and those that do use soft metrics that have nothing to do with profitability. Even attempting to determine what these costs are is frowned upon by scientists in the heavily converged fields of social science. Nevertheless, researchers have consistently found that there are statistical differences in both productivity and job attendance between various identity groups, and that a diverse workforce is a less efficient, less productive one.

And, obviously, workers who are not working are not being productive.

At the law firm of Faegre & Benson, 13 of the firm's 494 lawyers spent a combined 2,013 hours in meetings of the diversity committee discussing "furtherance of the firm's diversity initiatives", which does not include the time spent on frequent discussion of diversity topics at firm meetings, annual programming to highlight diversity issues, and targeted diversity training. At the U.S. Geological Survey, all managers are required to undergo four hours of diversity training every year.

A summary of the estimated effects of these four convergence-imposed costs on the corporation, based on anecdotal evidence as well as reviewing a number of published, peer-reviewed papers is as follows:

- 0.5 percent: time spent not working
- 12 to 30 percent: nonproductive employees
- 20 percent: reduced effectiveness of productive employees
- 5 percent: friction

It's important to remember that these costs are stackable, so the net effect of corporate convergence is to reduce the company's productivity by as much as 55 percent.

In other words, the average converged corporation is devoting a substantial portion of its annual budget to offending its customers in its core market, reducing the size of its client base, and significantly reducing the productivity of its workers. And to make matters worse, many corporations are turning over executive responsibility for corporate strategy to the very individuals responsible for imposing these costs on the corporation.

Want to cut your company's costs? Eliminate convergence. Is your company struggling with declining sales? Eliminate convergence. Want to double your company's productivity? Eliminate convergence.

There is only one cure for corporate cancer. Cut it out!

# Chapter 4
## Virtue-Signals and Warning Signs

Long before a corporation becomes completely converged, there are frequently signs that the danger zone is being entered. These warning signs tend to take the form of negative PR events that are often triggered by activity within the corporation on the part of its employees who are social justice advocates. While these events are usually seen as one-offs, and the negative consequences of them are invariably dismissed by the press and the corporate executives as mere happenstance, industry trends, or something else that has nothing to do with the actual cause, it is very important to recognize them as a sign that the corporation is in danger.

The National Football League's response to the anthem demonstrations is very typical in this regard. Despite the fact that the negative reactions to the decision of Colin Kaepernick and Eric Reid to kneel during the national anthem were loud, immediate, and measurable, it took nearly eighteen months for the league to admit that there was any relationship between the observable decline in its television ratings and the political demonstrations that angered and offended a portion of its core fan base.

Target Corporation's response to the controversy sparked by the announcement of its decision to permit transgendered men to use the women's bathrooms in its stores is also very illustrative in this regard.

On April 19, 2016, an unknown party posted a statement called "Continuing to Stand for Inclusivity" on *A Bullseye View*, the blog that serves as Target's public online voice.

> *Recent debate around proposed laws in several states has reignited a national conversation around inclusivity. So earlier this week, we reiterated with our team members where Target stands and how our beliefs are brought to life in how we serve our guests.*
>
> *Inclusivity is a core belief at Target. It's something we celebrate. We stand for equality and equity, and strive to make our guests and team members feel accepted, respected and welcomed in our stores and workplaces every day.*
>
> *We believe that everyone—every team member, every guest, and every community—deserves to be protected from discrimination, and treated equally. Consistent with this belief, Target supports the federal Equality Act, which provides protections to LGBT individuals, and opposes action that enables discrimination.*
>
> *In our stores, we demonstrate our commitment to an inclusive experience in many ways. Most relevant for the conversations currently underway, we welcome transgender team members and guests to use the restroom or fitting room facility that corresponds with their gender identity.*
>
> *We regularly assess issues and consider many factors such as impact to our business, guests and team members. Given the specific questions these legislative proposals raised about how we manage our fitting rooms and restrooms, we felt it was important to state our position.*
>
> *Everyone deserves to feel like they belong. And you'll always be accepted, respected and welcomed at Target.*
>
> *Tags: corporate responsibility, diversity, inclusion, LGBT Community, corporate social responsibility, inclusivity*

The post also featured a Target logo half-transformed into the rainbow that symbolizes gay pride.

However, the new policy announced in the post had not been approved by Target's CEO, Brian Cornell. Cornell later told *The Wall Street Journal* that he didn't even know about it until after the scandal broke, and said he would not have approved the decision to flaunt the controversial new policy in the faces of Target's unsuspecting customers. But, more importantly, the Target CEO also did not revoke the policy.

This is a classic example of an internal convergence coup, in which an individual employee manages to change his employer's public policy by unilateral action that is not approved by the organization's management.

The reaction of Target's largely female customer base to the announcement was loud, immediate, and specific. Women, particularly mothers with children, were extremely unhappy at the possibility of being subjected to men hanging around the ladies room and potentially being accosted by them. More than 1.5 million people, most of them women, signed a pledge to stop shopping at Target until the policy was reversed, which led to an immediate decline in shopper traffic, same-store sales, and Target's stock price.

One year later, *Business Insider UK* reported that Target "sales fell nearly 6% in the three quarters after the post compared with the same period last year, and same-store sales have dropped every quarter since the post."

In addition to losing $3.9 billion in sales, Target also wound up having to spend $20 million in order to install single-occupancy bathrooms in all its stores to permit its female customers to continue doing exactly what they had been doing before the new inclusivity policy was announced, which is going to the bathroom without having to share the space with self-identified ex-men. But did the Target executives learn anything from the experience? Apparently not.

"We took a stance, and we are going to continue to embrace our belief of diversity and inclusion," Cornell later told CNBC in an interview.

To be fair, Target's executives were hardly alone in failing to learn that virtue-signaling seldom pays.

In January 2017, in response to an executive order issued by the newly elected U.S. President to temporarily prevent refugees from entering the United States and ban entry for citizens from seven Muslim countries, the CEO of Starbucks, Howard Schultz, announced that the company would hire 10,000 refugees over the next five years. Supporters of the President immediately announced a boycott, and by July, Starbucks was forced to cut its revenue forecasts while enduring the biggest decline in its stock price in years.

Schultz himself resigned as CEO in June 2018, but not until the coffee chain engaged in a counterproductive and much-mocked exercise in corporate virtue-signaling that set a new standard for public self-abasement.

*More than 8,000 Starbucks coffee shops in the US closed their doors for racial bias training on Tuesday, in what the company said "isn't a solution, it's a first step" as it sought to rebuild its damaged reputation. Coffee shops across the country shut down in the early afternoon, as Starbucks walked 175,000 employees through a carefully designed training program on "understanding racial bias and the history of public accommodations in the United States".*

—"Starbucks closes more than 8,000 US cafes for racial bias training", *The Guardian*, May 29, 2018.

Starbucks paid a heavy cost for its virtue-signaling. The cost of the one-day chain-wide closure was estimated to be $12 million. This followed a 2017 that was marked by its worst sales performance in years, as its annual revenue growth fell 60 percent short of its three-year-average of 12.7 percent. That shortfall amounted to $1.63 billion less in sales than had been reasonably anticipated by investors, which is why, despite the historic stock market highs of 2017, the coffee chain's stock price is still lower than it was when Schultz made his ill-considered decision to weigh in on U.S. immigration policy.

And while one might think its position on U.S. immigration would have at least helped Starbucks with its international customers, two large Muslim groups in Malaysia and Indonesia, with 29.5 million members between them, are actually boycotting Starbucks themselves due to the corporation's very public support for LGBT rights.

Despite the danger that taking public stances on political positions obviously entails, both corporate executives and the business media continue to deny that there is any connection between these unpopular stances and the business consequences that tend to reliably follow them.

*We have made it clear over time that we've seen no material impact to the business based on the bathroom policy. We don't have anything new or different to share.*

—Erika Winkels, Public Relations Manager, Target

This stubborn denial of the observable cause is remarkably common in converged corporations. For example, the decline in NFL viewership was first blamed on the presidential election, then on a supposed lack of competitive games, and finally, on cord-cutting on the part of the audience. The idea that football fans might actually be turning off the games like they said they would simply didn't bear serious consideration.

Cord-cutting was also the explanation for an even more serious decline in ESPN viewers at the heavily converged sports network. ESPN, which now seems to devote more airtime to talking about politics than talking about sports, has been losing nearly one million subscribers every six months for the last seven years, and lost 480,000 in October

2017 alone. While cord-cutting is certainly a significant factor in their shrinking subscriber base, it does not suffice to explain all of their subscriber losses or their declining ratings.

The reduced number of Target shoppers was blamed on Amazon and other online options, while the fact that Walmart's traffic had not similarly declined was explained away by Walmart's less-confusing grocery options. Marvel's declining sales are presently being blamed on the comics giant "maximizing revenues from reboots, press-hyped events, variants and other collector-catnip" and "not the more talked-about issues of changing up established characters in the name of diversity."

While Marvel's convergence and subsequent decline in comics sales has not yet affected the popularity of movies produced by Disney-owned Marvel Studios, the signs of a future convergence-related decline are already there. Following the box office success of diversity flagship *Black Panther*, studio head Kevin Feige declared diversity and inclusion would henceforth be the studio's primary objectives.

> *Feige pointed specifically to Ryan Coogler's smash hit "Black Panther" for proof that Marvel moviegoers are eager for new stories made by diverse talents. "As audiences stay with us and audiences keep telling us, as they certainly did all around the world with 'Black Panther,' that they're embracing new ideas and new visions and new places and new ways of telling stories, we will just continue to grow and build on that," Feige said.*
>
> *As conversations in the industry regarding a greater desire for diversity and inclusion have started to produce results, Feige said he was confident that the MCU will be able to keep pace, and noted that the success of "Black Panther" and the excitement around "Captain Marvel" are indicative of those aims....*
>
> *"I think it's only the beginning," Feige said. "I think you'll see more and more of that in front of the camera, behind the camera and that that is what is required of us as storytellers. I think there's a lot to*

*pull from from the existing comics that they've been doing that for many, many years. Certainly with the support of Bob Iger and Alan Horn at Disney, we want these movies to reflect the world in which they are made, and be brought to life by all types of people behind the camera."*

—"Kevin Feige on Inclusion: Marvel Movies Are Now 'Required' to 'Reflect the World in Which They Are Made'", *Indiewire*, April 23, 2018.

No doubt everyone will be shocked and surprised when Marvel Studios suddenly begins to go into the same sort of unexpected decline without warning that Marvel Comics, *Star Wars*, Starbucks, the NFL, and NASCAR already have.

So, how can you identify if convergence is metastasizing in your organization? We'll address that in the next chapter.

# Chapter 5

## Diagnosing Convergence

Once you're convinced of the deadly dangers that convergence poses to the corporate bottom line, one obvious question occurs: how can you tell if your corporation is converged? And how badly is it already converged? Is it possible to determine how far along the convergence process it is, and can the process still be reversed?

The most effective way to diagnose a corporation is to compare its current state with those of well-known public companies at various states of convergence. For example, you may have happened to notice that the converged companies previously mentioned tended to share certain characteristics that are readily identifiable.

A heavily converged company will tend to feature the following traits:

- a recent peak in its most significant metric, be it popularity, influence, or revenue;
- a perception of the unassailability of its position in the market;
- an increased focus on issues unrelated to its core business, particularly on the part of the executives and marketing department;
- a public commitment to diversity, inclusivity, equality, or some other social justice cause;
- unqualified minorities employed in high-visibility executive positions;

- an observable intolerance for a diversity of opinions, especially those related to politics and religion;
- a chief executive who is a diva and enjoys putting himself into the public spotlight, especially for political reasons;
- an administration-heavy employee base;
- open contempt for its core audience;
- actively driving away its customers and clients.

If you work for practically any medium or large company in America, you might be having a bit of a panic attack after reading that list of symptoms. It's a little like visiting WebMD for the first time to figure out why you have the sniffles only to come away convinced you are suffering from an extremely rare form of stage four cancer.

Take a deep breath, not all is necessarily lost. Every company beyond small organizations tightly controlled by a strong CEO are to some degree converged. Convergence is part of corporate life. Think about germs—even human environments that strive to be as sterile as possible, like hospitals, still have germ problems, it's a fact of life on earth. The key to diagnosing heavy or full convergence, the true corporate cancers, is to put the traits and symptoms you witness in their proper context.

Overreaction to a low level of convergence can be as bad as ignoring the topic altogether. If a corporate newsletter virtue-signaling the hiring of a female engineer sends you into a spasm of outrage and fear, you will quickly devolve into a late-stage Howard Hughes, who shuffled around his Las Vegas penthouse wearing tissue boxes for shoes and bottling his urine for analysis.

We also run the risk of over-analysis in constantly trying to judge the convergence level of our organization. This too can be counterproductive as our time is spent judging just how badly our company has devoted itself to unprofitable leftist pipe dreams. In the consulting world, this common situation is referred to as "paralysis by analysis" and must be avoided to not exacerbate the negative effects of convergence itself.

Perhaps in the future, if scientists ever get grants to study topics besides climate change and the great benefits of diversity and multiculturalism, they will create a quantitative analysis framework for determining the convergence level of a corporation. We will be able to give every organization in the country a convergence score, and the scale will be logarithmic like the Richter scale—for those readers not science-minded, that means each level in the scale isn't one step more severe than the last, its *ten times worse.*

Until such time as scoring exists, we must rely on contextual examples to weigh to what extent our organization has surrendered to the madness of convergence. As I have stated, I doubt strongly that any organization of considerable size, especially public companies, will demonstrate a complete lack of convergence or only the first stage, infiltration.

Large companies are fertile soil for several of the traits of convergence I've listed. For example, consider the typical *Fortune 500* administration-heavy employee base. The larger the company, the more administrators, levels of management, and red tape it usually has. Social justice activists live for administration and red tape, as it suits their petty malevolence well and helps them avoid the consequences of their natural lack of productivity. The bigger the company, the more administrators, and the more administrators, the more convergence there tends to be.

Another common trait is a very vocal and public commitment to diversity, inclusivity, equality, or some other social justice cause. There is nary a single major corporation that doesn't embrace this. Just look at the social media posts of your favorite major brand during gay pride month. Clearly there is a widespread belief on the part of marketing executives that social justice pandering of this sort is good marketing. And that may even be true, depending, of course, on the specific market involved.

Marketing in all its forms is pandering to one degree or another. The marketing department's job is to figure out the best way to sell its products to consumers throughout the market. Consumers aren't one consistent block, but an extremely complex web of often-interlocking subgroups. Figuring out who these different groups are and marketing to their particular preferences is called segmentation. It relies on the correct belief that not all consumers react to advertising the same way and it has become a requirement of modern business to not only identify consumer groups, but to create ads and marketing materials elaborately tailored to these groups.

This trend is effectively mocked in the popular clip from the *Tim and Eric Awesome Show, Great Job!* skit titled "Free Real Estate". Social media has turned the catchphrase "free real estate" into a meme, but the real point of the skit is the beginning of the fake commercial, which indicates it is aimed at one person: "The following advertisement is intended for Jim Boonie only." This is segmentation in its most extreme form.

While one of the key infiltration points for convergence is the marketing department, it is important to understand that not everything that looks like convergence is necessarily indicative of corporate cancer eating away at the organization. This is why it is useful to develop a metric capable of distinguishing genuine convergence from good old-fashioned marketing to a particular market segment.

There are several standard characteristics that apply to a broad range of market segments. Some consumers purchase products because the quality and value are the best. Many people believe they are part of this segment, but they actually just use the concept of value to rationalize purchases made for other reasons. A large segment of the population buys products out of brand loyalty, such as truck drivers who possess a strong preference for Chevy or Ford trucks. This is a highly valuable segment which is why most companies work hard to build brand loyalty.

Increasingly, many Americans make purchases that make them feel good. That is where social justice marketing most often fits in, as the corporate social justice activists assert that a rising percentage of the population will buy a product primarily because they want to signal their identification with a company that hires disabled transgendered individuals as their television models or features a happy family of multiracial homosexuals in their commercials.

As a quick example of segmentation in action, think about what we see from fast food chain Wendy's. A lot of their advertising focuses on their food quality and how tasty it is, like big pictures of juicy burgers in their window. They market to other segments through rapid introduction of products—like ghost pepper cheese sauce—to jump on bandwagons. Wendy's practically invented a new form of segmentation to young people with its snappy social media account which often mocks other brands and even customers. This account caused a considerable jump in sales as eating at Wendy's became a trend for young people. Does Wendy's have much advertising focused on social justice? Not particularly. They do have a campaign that pushes the real-life Wendy, which may be interpreted as a "women in leadership" campaign if one stretches the concept a bit, but is better attributed to brand integrity—Dave Thomas named the company after her!

However, as an example of apparent social justice activism that is not necessarily convergence, consider the craze for lavender advertising that tries to sneak in a homosexual couple in everything from cat food to mortgage ads. While gays and lesbians only represent about two percent of the population, they are an enticing market segment since they tend to be status-conscious consumers with no children and no shortage of disposable cash. As soon as marketers figured out that catering to this segment by virtue-signaling was all they needed to do to win it over, they knew they had found an ideal consumer segment on which they could push a constant stream of products. Indeed, for many gays and lesbians, a rainbow flag on social media is all it takes to pick up a loyal, life-long customer.

So, the temptation to engage in a little cheap virtue-signaling is understandable. The problem, of course, is that there is a declining marginal utility to it, especially for those organizations that are market followers. Subaru already owns its target market, so there isn't much benefit to waving the rainbow flag to other automotive manufacturers competing with it. And then, the lack of wisdom inherent in make a public show of signaling to a one small segment while offending other, much larger segments should be obvious to everyone who understands how to divide from 100.

The key to distinguishing between genuine segment-signaling and its converged virtue-signaling counterpart is whether the segment being signaled is actually a significant part of the consumer base for the product being advertised or not. A rainbow flag on travel agency selling gay cruises is not an indication of convergence. A rainbow flag on children's toothpaste almost certainly is.

In any event, the marketing department is where you are advised to begin your investigation of a corporation's convergence. Marketing is how companies communicate to the rest of the world how they want to be seen and for what they want to be known. It's a portal to the psyche of the organization, and is also one of the primary doorways for convergence to take root.

Marketing is also the first public indication that a company has gone off the rails by losing touch with its customers and what made the company successful in the first place. The problem is that the rest of the organization relies chiefly upon the marketing department to determine what the consumers in the marketplace want. If you are an operations manager in a meeting and the marketing manager tells you that customers are demanding the replacement of the company's plastic straws with paper ones to save the world, who are you to argue? You may know that paper straws are more expensive and tend to fall apart when used in hot drinks. You may also know that switching to paper straws will hurt the company's profit margins and contribute to dissatisfied customers or even the next round of layoffs. But the marketing department will tell you that it knows what the customer wants, and the customer is always right!

The problem with converged marketing departments begins when the employee informing the rest of the organization about what its customers want doesn't actually know or care what the customers' real needs are, but only care what signals their virtue or pushes their political agenda.

In the interest of helping you more accurately gauge the level of convergence in your organization or in one of the companies with whom you work, it may be useful to consider the current state of several large corporations with which you may be familiar.

## Chick-fil-A

The popular chicken restaurant chain has nearly 2,000 restaurants and still respects the values of its Southern Baptist founder. All of its restaurants are closed on Sundays as well as on Thanksgiving and Christmas. The company has in the past donated to Christian organizations that oppose the formal government recognition of same-sex relationships, and successfully withstood boycott attempts as well as liberal politicians seeking to ban its expansion into Boston and Chicago. It has a stated philosophy of refusing to support organizations with political agendas and has not altered its corporate policies despite external pressure to do so.

*Verdict*: Unconverged.

## Discover Financial Services

Discover has been pushing diversity as hard as it does its credit cards. It constantly runs ads on social media platforms pushing its equality initiatives and inclusivity. One video features a wide range of ambiguously-sexed employees discussing how great it is to work for Discover. These ads are so common you'd be forgiven for thinking Discover was an easy example of a fully-converged company about to go down in flames.

Although its marketing is heavy on the social justice, the company is not. Discover is a tightly-run ship that has earned great brand loyalty through excellent customer service including using only domestic call centers. Your calls to Discover are never answered by a person named "Billy" with an indecipherable accent. They are at the top of their game, with record revenues and profits for the third quarter of 2019 just reported as of the time of this writing.

*Verdict*: Lightly converged. Despite a strong degree of convergence in the marketing department, Discover remains considerably less converged at the overall company level, and has demonstrated the core competencies it requires to resist further convergence.

## Ford Motor Company

Ford presents a considerable amount of social justice pandering in its marketing. The tour for a Ford manufacturing facility, like the mighty River Rouge Complex in Detroit, spends as much time on its use of renewable energy and the fact that grass is grown on the roof of the plant as it does on how it puts cars together. It is of particular concern that the company is advertising the fact that the chief engineer on its all-electric F-150 pickup truck is a Chinese woman named Linda Zhang.

For all its green pandering, Ford remains a profitable car company that dominates the truck market by producing superior products that continue to appeal to its core customer base. It is the only major U.S. automaker that wasn't bailed out with tax dollars after the financial crisis of 2008. Turning Zhang into the star of its electric truck unveiling is an annoyance, but only time will tell if it leads to the convergence-caused disaster of introducing a bad truck to the market. Ford has had terrible cars before—never forget the Edsel—but a bad truck when you dominate the truck space would be a really stupid move.

The electric truck product is not, in itself, a sign of convergence. Ford would be silly not to explore this technology, and they are doing so by emphasizing what their traditional customer market wants: torque and pulling capacity. Electric vehicles also have the added benefit of helping the company meet the government's restrictive pollution laws.

*Verdict*: Moderately converged, about average for a large U.S. corporation

## Intel

The premier U.S. manufacturer of semiconductor chips has fully embraced social justice at the same time it has fallen behind its foreign and domestic competitors in terms of both sales and technology. It has a diversity initiative encouraging diversity interest groups among its employees as well as its suppliers and has repeatedly received a 100 percent rating from the Corporate Equality Index published by the largest LGBTQ political lobbying organization in the United States. It also releases an annual Global Diversity & Inclusion report and invested $300 million in an attempt to enhance gender and racial diversity in their own company as well as the technology industry as a whole.

The former market leader is now multiple generations behind its competitors, as its planned 2016 move from a 14-nanometer process to a 10-nm process was delayed for three years while AMD and Samsung are already producing 7-nm products.

*Verdict*: Heavily converged.

Through systematically examining various corporate examples such as these, it will quickly become apparent that convergence is not simply a matter of public appearances or advertising campaigns. Convergence isn't simply a matter of corporate marketing positioning, it concerns the way in which the leadership of the organization has bought into the social justice madness to the point of no return, thereby causing the organization to lose the ability to perform its primary functions, to ignore its declining revenues and profits, and to refuse to listen to the complaints of the company's traditional customer base.

# Chapter 6

## Why Full Convergence is Fatal

Convergence happens gradually over time, so it's not uncommon for those who work in corporate America to suddenly find themselves caught up in it like the proverbial frog in the pot who didn't notice the temperature changing until the water started boiling.

However, combining a bit of intelligent observation with the knowledge that has been shared here, you'll soon find that both heavily- and fully-converged organizations will stick out like a sore thumb. Or, as the case may be, like a black and rotting one.

Like earthquakes and other natural disasters, the catastrophe of full corporate convergence is logarithmic in nature. Heavy convergence is ten times worse than moderate convergence, and full convergence is ten times worse than that. You don't need to be a full-time culture warrior to recognize full convergence, because its consequences make it all but inescapable to anyone who is not willfully blind.

The more heavily converged the company, the more of the symptoms laid out in the previous chapters will be exhibited. But it isn't only a matter of how many symptoms are present, or even necessarily their severity. Full convergence dictates that the business begins to actively act against its best interests, purposefully poisoning its relationships with its customers, with its shareholders, and with its employees alike. Final-stage convergence acts very much like a metastasized cancer inside the corporation, being simultaneously an integral part of the body as well as a mortal threat to its continued existence.

That additional factor of openly acting against the interests of its customers and the company itself is a key identifier for the heavily converged organizations. One of the most obvious indicators to quickly determine the level of convergence is the attitude and actions of the company's Chief Executive Officer. The CEO is, after all, the leader of the whole organization. If a CEO is personally committed to social justice or has been converged by his subordinates, it's safe to assume the entire organization is fully converged or will be soon.

Whenever possible, compare a CEO you suspect of being converged to one who is not. Develop a control group of companies and CEOs in different industries that are not heavily converged, and compare their actions with those of the executives at your organization or the company in question.

Take, for example, Oracle Corporation co-founder Larry Ellison, who eventually stepped down as CEO but has remained deeply involved as its Chief Technology Officer. Despite making billions in the progressive heart of Silicon Valley, Ellison has remained remarkably clean of convergence. He is a notorious diva who lives in a faux-Japanese castle, practices Samurai swordsmanship, and is well known for Oracle's hard-sell tough negotiation style. But he never turned his company against its customers and employees, he spent a career ruthlessly weeding out non-performers from his company (which naturally protected it from convergence) and never treated his customers with the utter contempt that is a hallmark of Silicon Valley companies today.

In today's Silicon Valley, a place that features includes Google selling its soul to communist China, Facebook selling every detail of your life to the highest bidder, and Twitter transforming itself from the "free speech wing of the free speech party" into the "censorship wing of the fascist party", Oracle and Larry Ellison almost look like good guys by comparison, which no doubt would have astonished many a tech insider from yesteryear.

Compare Ellison's behavior with the antics of T-Mobile CEO John

Legere. Legere's social media presence makes it look as if he is having a particularly absurd midlife crisis. He seems to believe he can pass for one of the cool kids by adopting the culture and the politics of the wokest youth. The business world is rarely more amusing than Internet memes, but Legere is a walking "How do you do, fellow kids?" meme writ large.

A goofy CEO acting like a teenager on social media could be written off as putting a spin on the successful Wendy's social media marketing gambit if it wasn't paired with disastrous business decisions that put politics and social justice virtue-signaling ahead of customer service and business savvy.

T-Mobile and Legere showed their true level of convergence during the 2018 Super Bowl. The NFL championship game is widely considered the biggest TV advertising event in the world, with companies paying major bucks to unveil new products or debut ads so quirky and creative that they stick in the minds of millions of viewers. T-Mobile took to that stage to preach the social justice gospel of equality.

Think about that for a moment. Who else besides a collection of fully-converged corporate idiots would go to the Super Bowl, an event that skews heavily male and conservative, to preach a social justice message about society's supposed inequality and gender problems? Did the T-Mobile advertising department think that woke Twitter feminists and transsexual Marxist studies majors take a break once a year from their cancel-culture antics in order to watch the Super Bowl?

Here is how the *Wall Street Journal* described T-Mobile's ad during the big game:

> *The spot pans across close-ups of babies from diverse backgrounds as actress Kerry Washington offers them motivational life advice.*
>
> *"Some people may see your differences and be threatened by them," Ms. Washington intones. "But you are unstoppable. You'll love who you want. You'll demand fair and equal pay. You will not allow where you come from to dictate where you're going."*

Who on Earth imagined this was a good idea for a Super Bowl ad? A fully-converged company run by a fully-converged CEO, of course.

The *Journal* included an explanation from T-Mobile's advertising honcho that could come from any college feminist: " 'Brands have an important role in changing culture,' said Nick Drake, executive vice president of marketing at T-Mobile. The company created the ad to 'spark more conversation' about equality in hopes that it can help 'drive permanent change on the subject matter,' he added."

Legere himself defended the much-criticized ads on his personal social media accounts, again using the language more customarily seen from gender-confused bluehairs featuring preferred pronouns in their bio: "@TMobile has always stood for inclusivity, equality & the idea that we can change things for good. One thing I know is that change doesn't just happen. It requires people to join together."

Now, T-Mobile is a relatively minor example of full convergence. They are not in a position of dominance in the cell service market, and both their customers and their employees can readily flee to Verizon and other competitors as Legere's converged company inevitably devolves into a cesspit of diversity hires, declining sales, technological stasis, and terrible service.

You don't need to look far in the tech sector, especially in Silicon Valley, to find examples of fully converged organizations. Many, if not most of the prominent Internet companies you can think of are heavily or fully converged. Perhaps the most converged of all is Google. Google.com is the number one website on the entire Internet. Many people don't realize that the company also controls the number two site, YouTube.

Google is riddled with the type of far-left progressive politics you'd expect from Silicon Valley. Breitbart News released a transcript of a leaked company meeting that took place after the election of President Donald Trump featuring top executives choking back tears over the unexpected defeat of Hillary Clinton as well as others who sounded more like speakers at a Democratic Socialists of America meeting on campus than corporate professionals.

Nor should it surprise anyone that the company was caught conspiring with the Chinese government to create a censored search engine for the country that would simultaneously keep citizens in the dark while exposing enemies of the Communist Party. The company swears to this day that "Project Dragonfly" has been scrapped, but only time will tell. For soulless globalists at Google who considered Hillary Clinton their ideal president, deception and misdirection are the way to do business.

If you peel back Google's surface progressivism, you will expose a nightmare of full convergence. The most extreme forms of identity politics are part of the everyday experience at Google. For example, even the men's restrooms feature tampons because "some men menstruate".

Satire simply can't keep pace with the nonsensical shenanigans that take place inside a fully-converged corporation. For example, one Google employee who sexually identifies as "a yellow-scaled wingless dragonkin" while simultaneously identifying as an "expansive ornate building" presented a talk entitled "Living as a Plural Being" at a company event for xir's coworkers.

In a sane world, this sort of behavior would see you committed to an institution to prevent you from injuring yourself. At Google, this is the sort of thing that puts you on the fast track for promotion.

Google is at the bleeding edge of convergence culture thanks to its HR department, which, as you now know, is a primary infiltration point for social justice warriors. At Google, the HR department acts as the company's Gestapo.

One of an HR department's primary roles in any organization is to prevent the company from being sued for employee rights violations under State and federal labor laws. But at Google, HR's primary job is to make excuses for SJWs, promote "diversity," and silence any crypto-conservatives who somehow got past them in the interview process. We began to witness this in 2015, when a rogue Google employee brought evidence of serious harassment and discrimination against conservatives, men, and Caucasians to the attention of Google HR. Google HR simply made excuses for the progressive activists despite their repeated violations of the company's code of conduct and ignored their unprofessional behavior, thus ensuring nothing was done about the systemic problem with Google's corporate culture.

Consider this snippet from another complaint lodged the same year:

*On or around August 2015, Adam Fletcher ("Fletcher"), a L6 SRE Manager at Google, Jake McGuire ("McGuire"), a L7 SRE Manager at Google, and Nori Heikkinen ("Heikkinen"), a L6 SRE Manager at Google all publicly endorsed blacklisting conservatives and actively preventing them from seeking employment opportunities at Google. Google's management-sanctioned blacklists were directed at specific Google employees who tactfully expressed conservative viewpoints in politically-charged debates. In one case, Jay Gengelbach, a L6 SWE Manager, publicly bragged about blacklisting an intern for failing to change his conservative views. Kim Burchett ("Burchett"), a L7 SWE Manager, proposed creating an online company-wide blacklist of political conservatives inside Google.*

In 2016, conservative blogger Curtis Yarvin visited Google's campus as a guest to have lunch with an employee. Yarvin's name turned out to be on a secret HR blacklist, raising a silent alarm on his arrival. He was located by security and escorted off the campus. Other people on the blacklist include Alex Jones, and, it will probably not surprise you to learn, this author. As Breitbart News exposed in a leaked email chain, one Google employee wrote "We have tons of white- and blacklists that humans manually curate. Hopefully this isn't surprising or particularly controversial."

Google, like any police state, is heavily occupied with creating black-lists and enacting bans, acting as speech and thought police for its users and employees alike.

The world learned just how converged Google had become after employee James Damore published his famous memo on an internal message boards. The memo included Damore's belief that while the company celebrated racial, sexual, orientational, and, apparently, species diversity, it sorely lacked anything in the way of ideological diversity, as it heavily enforced leftist groupthink instead. Damore also made a number of points that were solidly based on scientific evidence and other data, such as the fact that women are disproportionately unsuited for and uninterested in many STEM jobs. To Google's closet conservatives, the Damore memo came as a breath of fresh air. But to many of Google's employees, particularly the most converged ones, it appeared to be the final sign of the apocalypse.

*How could such a horribly bigoted misogynist work for Google?*

This demarcation was apparent in media coverage of the Damore memo once it went public. Conservative media called it a "viewpoint diversity memo", while the mainstream media and leftist tech sites used a variety of different terms for the document, with more than a few describing it as a "manifesto" in an attempt to associate it with the Unabomber's screed and various other writings by scary white men.

Almost immediately after the memo became public, Google CEO Sundar Pichai published his own response to the memo. Pichai's response is worth including here in full, in order to truly understand the degree of the internal backlash against a memo that basically said "Hey, maybe you might want some diversity in how people think, too."

One thing that must be noted here is that Pichai is little more than a puppet CEO. The real power is the social justice hivemind at Alphabet Inc., the self-appointed Masters of the Universe, who spun themselves off as a parent company to Google and its creepy sister companies like Waymo, Deepmind, and Sidewalk Labs.

Pichai's response, via the Google blog, was naturally published in the "diversity and inclusion" section.

*This has been a very difficult time. I wanted to provide an update on the memo that was circulated over this past week.*

*First, let me say that we strongly support the right of Googlers to express themselves, and much of what was in that memo is fair to debate, regardless of whether a vast majority of Googlers disagree with it. However, portions of the memo violate our Code of Conduct and cross the line by advancing harmful gender stereotypes in our workplace. Our job is to build great products for users that make a difference in their lives. To suggest a group of our colleagues have traits that make them less biologically suited to that work is offensive and not OK. It is contrary to our basic values and our Code of Conduct, which expects "each Googler to do their utmost to create a workplace culture that is free of harassment, intimidation, bias and unlawful discrimination."*

*The memo has clearly impacted our co-workers, some of whom are hurting and feel judged based on their gender. Our co-workers shouldn't have to worry that each time they open their mouths to speak in a meeting, they have to prove that they are not like the memo states, being "agreeable" rather than "assertive," showing a "lower stress tolerance," or being "neurotic."*

*At the same time, there are co-workers who are questioning whether they can safely express their views in the workplace (especially those with a minority viewpoint). They too feel under threat, and that is also not OK. People must feel free to express dissent. So to be clear again, many points raised in the memo—such as the portions criticizing Google's trainings, questioning the role of ideology in the workplace, and debating whether programs for women and underserved groups are sufficiently open to all—are important topics. The author had a right to express their views on those topics—we encourage an environment in which people can do this and it remains our policy to not take action against anyone for prompting these discussions.*

*The past few days have been very difficult for many at the company, and we need to find a way to debate issues on which we might disagree—while doing so in line with our Code of Conduct.*

*I'd encourage each of you to make an effort over the coming days to reach out to those who might have different perspectives from your own. I will be doing the same.*

*I have been on work related travel in Africa and Europe the past couple of weeks and had just started my family vacation here this week. I have decided to return tomorrow as clearly there's a lot more to discuss as a group—including how we create a more inclusive environment for all.*

There are a few key things to note in this reply, beside the fact that it demonstrates the Google CEO's fluency in the purest form of SJW-speak, one that is rarely seen outside college campuses and Twitter.

First, notice that Pichai mentions Google's Code of Conduct several times. In high-tech organizations, particularly open source projects, codes of conduct are the extremists' primary weapon for ejecting project members who are unwilling to submit to the social justice narrative. For example, it only took one year from the time that Linus Torvalds relaxed his benevolent dictatorship over Linux and permitted the Linux Foundation to install a code of conduct that subscribes to the lunatic principles of the Contributor Covenant created by a transgender activist before programmers were being banned from Linux Foundation events for the crime of being pictured in a pro-Trump hat.

There are a variety of ways activists manipulate these pernicious codes of conduct to police thought and speech, but for the most part they favor applying selective enforcement by ignoring serious violations committed by the approved while punishing invented ones on the part of the unauthorized. Consider this portion of Damore's legal complaint:

> *On August 3, 2017 George Sadlier ("Sadlier"), a Director at Google, sent out a mass email condemning James' essay as "repulsive and intellectually dishonest" and promising an HR investigation into Damore. Sadlier also promoted posts that advocated for physical violence against Damore. Subsequently, On Friday, August 4, 2017, Damore received a late-night email from Alex Hidalgo, a Site Reliability Engineer at Google in Sadlier's organization, which stated, "You're a misogynist and a terrible person. I will keep hounding you until one of us is fired. Fuck you."*

When viewed in the light of Pichai's stress on the importance of Google's Code of Conduct, does the behavior of either of these relatively high-ranking employees appear to be in line with the policy that requires "each Googler to do their utmost to create a workplace culture that is free of harassment, intimidation, bias and unlawful discrimination?"

At most less-converged companies, HR would see its responsibilities lay with protecting the organization from its egregiously misbehaving employees, and take immediate action against any individual threatening a coworker with serial harassment. At any corporation where professional behavior was expected, issuing threats like this would soon result in being frog-marched to the front door by security and told not to come back again. At Google, it quickly became a contest to see who could signal their virtue most violently by attacking Damore and other conservative coworkers.

Google, like many companies, has a system of peer rewards that allow coworkers to nominate individuals for a small bonus to recognize their hard work, outstanding service, or going above and beyond their job duties. Believe it or not, the response of Google HR department to the attacks on Damore was to approve nominating employees for peer rewards on the basis of publicly attacking the man's politics and his character!

The mass of the converged inside Google spoke with a single voice, as they often do, and their message was straightforward. Damore was a marked man. They wanted his head and they wanted it immediately! Needless to say, Damore didn't last long at Google after publishing his "anti-diversity manifesto". For all of Pichai's mealy-mouthed words about Google employees being free to speak their mind, Damore was fired three days after the leaked manifesto first went public on *Motherboard*.

The ex-Googler filed a lawsuit on the matter that was later joined by other white men but has since abandoned that suit and gone into private mediation with what may be most converged company in the world.

It is possible that some of you will be tempted to decide that all of this outrageous behavior is fine and nothing more than the free market at work. The problem here is that Google is silencing ideas of which its neofascistic hivemind disapproves outside the company to nearly the same extent that it does inside. And when a single company controls the number one search engine, the number one video platform, and is the larger partner in the online advertising duopoly, that silencing goes a long way.

This is laid bare in an internal presentation called "The Good Censor" that was originally meant only for Google eyes, but was leaked to *Breitbart News*. I encourage you to seek out the full presentation, which is full of chillingly censorious ideas Google believes are necessary for the future of the Internet. Here is just a small taste of what Breitbart reported:

> *The first approach is described as a product of the "American tradition" which "prioritizes free speech for democracy, not civility." The second is described as a product of the "European tradition," which*

*"favors dignity over liberty and civility over freedom." The briefing claims that all tech platforms are now moving toward the European tradition.*

*The briefing associates Google's new role as the guarantor of "civility" with the categories of "editor" and "publisher." This is significant, given that Google, YouTube, and other tech giants publicly claim they are not publishers but rather neutral platforms—a categorization that grants them special legal immunities under Section 230 of the Communications Decency Act. Elsewhere in the document, Google admits that Section 230 was designed to ensure they can remain neutral platforms for free expression.*

Once a company reaches complete convergence, as Google has, the SJWs inside the organization will soon cease to even bother hiding their total lack of interest in either the bottom line or the core business. Or, like Google, they think they can simply blacklist discussion of such minor inconveniences as the company's performance. For example, another heavily-converged tech giant, Apple, has ceased reported the number of iPhones it sells each quarter, which number was formerly considered a key metric to gauge the performance of the socially-conscious phone and computer giant.

Another common feature of fully-converged companies is to demonstrate open contempt for the very people whose business is required in order for the corporation to continue to operate. This is usually made most apparent in the entertainment industry.

Rian Johnson, the director of the disastrous *The Last Jedi*, openly asserted that his job was to "inevitably disappoint part of the fanbase that doesn't get just the thing it wants." Kathleen Kennedy, the Disney executive who is arguably the one individual most responsible for destroying the *Star Wars* brand, was equally dismissive of the franchise's core audience.

*I don't feel that I have a responsibility to cater in some way. I would never just seize on saying, 'Well, this is a franchise that's appealed primarily to men for many, many years, and therefore I owe men something.'*

—*"Star Wars*: Kathleen Kennedy Says She Doesn't Need To Cater To Male Fans", *Screenrant*, November 29, 2016

Notice that she made those comments well *before* Disney's three most recent *Star Wars* bombs. What Ms. Kennedy appears to have forgotten is that the male fans she disdains don't have a responsibility to support movies they don't want to see produced by people who don't care what appeals to them. That sort of contempt for the primary market has a way of filtering down through the organization, which is why it is a massive red flag when a top executive feels comfortable broadcasting such contemptuous indifference towards the company's core customers.

There is no question that customers most definitely notice the contempt in which they are held before they cease to be customers. For example, the following comment by one YouTuber is only one of tens of thousands of similar comments, reviews, rants, and diatribes by the hardcore *Star Wars* fans who were so cavalierly dismissed by the converged executives at Disney.

*The* Star Wars *prequel trilogy may have been poor-quality* Star Wars *films, but they still felt like* Star Wars *to me and it felt like we were in the* Star Wars *universe. These latest ones are something else completely, they are a complete abomination. I was also a massive* Star Wars *fan and read every book to the extended universe, played just about every game that came out. Watching that first new one was like someone threw up over my childhood memories. I certainly haven't watched one since.*

—Wrong Think, *YouTube*

One can find similar sentiments being expressed by the former fans, supporters, and customers of every single one of the companies that are mentioned in this book. These sentiments cannot be dismissed as normal customer dissatisfaction, because the anger, the grief, and the palpable sense of betrayal are unmistakable. Such customers, once lost, are not going to be easily regained. Among the many costs of convergence, one must count the loss of customer loyalty, brand reputation, and repeat business.

The primary idea behind this book is the assertion that social justice convergence is bad for business because it sacrifices revenue and customer relationships, and hinders the performance of otherwise productive employees. One common objection to this thesis is that many of the most converged companies, like the Silicon Valley giants, are too big to fail. In essence, the counterargument insists that some companies are so big and popular that no amount of political lunacy or indifference toward the consumer can hurt them.

But this simply is not true. No corporation is immortal, no organization is immune to failure, and no heavily converged company is going to escape its eventual fate brought about by the suboptimal decisions of its executives. No organization, no matter how dominant, can expect to survive incompetence forever.

Look at mighty Apple. Less than ten years after the death of Steve Jobs, Apple is already showing signs of hitting turbulence by their refusal to publish their iPhone sales numbers. Without the unique vision of Jobs to guide them, the once-excellent nature of its designs has devolved into adding spider-eyed cameras to the back of their phones and forcing a series of unnecessarily proprietary connections onto consumers. Has anyone seen my dongle? Why can't I just use my Bose headphones with my iPhone? Apple is still very healthy financially, but the magic is gone and it is now relying upon foreign markets for its growth, a development that renders it increasingly vulnerable in light of the trade war with China and other international economic disruptions.

What about big companies outside the tech sector? One of the best examples to consider is Starbucks. The coffee giant exploded from Seattle to reach nearly 30,000 locations around the globe, half of those opened in the last decade. Starbucks, like many of the most successful companies of all time, answered a question that consumers didn't even know they had: "Can I enjoy coffee with pretentious names and inflated prices while showing my urban and professional peers that I am of a similar status?"

Starbucks pushes progressive and social justice values along with its fancy coffee drinks and overpriced sandwiches. But what was once a progressive company with a strong corporate culture that put its energy into positive activities like compensating its employees well and providing them with solid benefits has evolved into a converged monster.

One of the first signs of the convergence of Starbucks is what has become an annual tradition of sparring between Christians and the company over its "holiday-themed" cups that go out of their way to avoid any connection to the actual Christmas holiday that most of its customers are cheerfully celebrating. Like all heavily-converged organizations, Starbucks has turned against its customers in a wide variety of ways. For example, it punished the staff of a store for ejecting loiterers who weren't purchasing anything, basing its decision solely on the race of the loiterers—they were black men—and Starbucks decided its staff was racist and wrong for treating black individuals in the same way they would treat other members of society. The company closed over 8,000 stores for a day of "racial bias training", and put a policy in place declaring that loiterers were welcome in its stores, including the bathrooms. Suddenly customers of all races and political persuasions were faced with the disgusting option of getting a drink at Starbucks and using a restroom filled with blood, needles, and God only knows what other messes left by homeless drug addicts and other undesirables invited by the company's new "open door" policy.

Starbucks has so many other convergence-driven policies that have been intensely unpopular with customers that they are hard to number. A personal favorite is the company's announcement in early 2017 that it would hire 10,000 refugees, an attempt to thumb its nose at President Donald Trump's sensible refugee policies, including the travel ban placed on select Muslim countries. To say that customers hated the new policy would understate the reaction. Starbucks eventually backed down, but the fact that the coffee giant would take a position on U.S. immigration in the first place defies both business and common sense.

Following its increasingly regular PR disasters, Starbucks has taken a significant financial hit. According to media reports, Starbucks is closing at least 150 stores in 2019 due to poor performance. This is a company that wouldn't have dreamed of needing to close any stores as recently as a few years ago, as its fancy coffees and milkshakes have been a license to print money for decades.

Don't make the mistake that companies like Walt Disney have by assuming that major entertainment properties are immune to suffering massive drops in sales as well. Twitter user @danev888 studied the Google trends data on *Star Wars* from 2004 to present and found interest in the franchise is at an all-time low. This is the precise opposite of what the media was predicting, since they believe women were left behind by *Star Wars* fandom until the recent feminist-friendly movies produced by Disney.

If SJWs can kill *Star Wars*, they certainly can kill whatever company you work for or with whom you do business. If your company is in an industry that possesses any sort of public prestige, be it tech, games, film, science, or media, they are likely trying to murder the market leaders even as you read these words.

This is a good point to explain why convergence goes beyond bad business into the category of being pure evil. Although there are some converged companies that are minor players in their industry, most prominent completely converged companies pair their over-the-rainbow SJW values with positions of market dominance. As we've illustrated with the T-Mobile example, customers unhappy with the SJW bent of the company can switch service to AT&T or Verizon, among other choices.  But such a switch is not so easy when the converged company possesses overwhelming market dominance, such as Facebook, Google, Intel, or Disney.

This dominance is listed as one of our traits of converged organizations, but we've downplayed it to this point. "A perception of the unassailability of its position in the market," means that at least internally, the converged company believes it can say and do whatever it likes, because you're stuck—you simply have no alternative.

The Walt Disney Company is the most powerful entertainment company on Earth.  Google is the Internet for a large percentage of consumers.  In many or most examples of fully converged companies, the company either has—or believes it has—a stranglehold on at least one segment of the market.  Otherwise its SJWs are relegated to keeping themselves partially in the shadows and making minor moves against traditional Western culture instead of the broad strokes we see from the converged.

Dick's Sporting Goods is the largest chain of its kind in America.  Dick's combined with e-commerce and Walmart has put most local and small-chain sporting goods stores out of business.  Local sporting goods shops used to be a fixture of every town, but now that they're gone, Dick's is free to flex its SJW muscles.  Following the Parkland school shootings, Dick's signaled its virtue by announcing massive changes to how the chain sells guns.  100 stores stopped selling guns altogether, and the rest of the chain put restrictions in place on customers under 21.  All Dick's stores stopped selling "assault rifles", and the company reportedly destroyed $5 million worth of such rifles, instead of returning them for vendor credit.  These changes have cost the chain $250 million in losses, which the CEO downplayed by saying, "some gun enthusiasts have stopped shopping at the chain."

Now that is a considerable understatement!

We can safely assume when Dick's was in tight competition with local and regional retailers, it put its energy into pleasing customers and providing the best products, services, and prices, instead of playing up its converged politics. After all, SJWs are not Dick's customers. They are not, to put it politely, known for their active lifestyles and interest in participating in organized sporting activities.

The evil of convergence becomes very apparent when comparing the behavior of converged companies before and after they reach a position of market dominance. There is some wiggle room in this argument because few organizations are fully converged at conception, but the comparison of how a position of market dominance brings SJW poison to the surface is quite revealing.

Going back to the tech sector, Google always positioned itself as the good guys, draping the company in the flag as it embraced freedom of speech and its infamous corporate motto of "Don't Be Evil." These days the corporate motto is gone, along with any pretense of not doing evil—whether it is spying on people for profit, cutting deals with communist China, harassing conservative employees out the door, or meddling in elections at home and abroad.

Twitter is a tiny company compared to Google, but it dominates its own niche of social media. Executives once proudly described the company as the "free speech wing of the free speech party," but where are they now? Twitter seems to put all of its energy into new technology to shadowban users and stop the viral spread of ideas it doesn't like, to the point where its ad software broke down, costing the company significant amounts of revenue and prompting an October 2019 lawsuit by shareholders based on the company's inept management. Oh, and the free speech wing of the free speech party? Company CEO Jack Dorsey addressed that in 2018, claiming it was a "joke", and not meant as a serious comment. The left can't meme and SJWs can't joke—this was a weak excuse at best.

Amazon is gradually following the same trend towards full convergence. On its way up, Amazon was a staunch defender of freedom. As recently as 2010, a company spokesperson said "it is censorship not to sell certain books simply because we or others believe their message is objectionable." In what would now be called a red-pilled addendum to its statement, Amazon said, "Amazon does not support or promote hatred or criminal acts, however, we do support the right of every individual to make their own purchasing decisions."

That is the Amazon of the past. The Amazon of the present bans books whenever a rogue employee feel offended by one and decide to target it. One book published by Castalia House, a satirical science fiction novel called *Corrosion*, was delisted by an employee in the Quality Assurance department no less than seven times despite the book being repeatedly determined by KDP managers to not violate their guidelines in any way and republished.

*Hello,*

*While reviewing the following books we found the title, cover image, descriptions and/or authors of the following book(s) are misleading to our customers:*

*Title: Corrosion (The Corroding Empire Book 1)*

*As a result, the book(s) have been removed from sale from Amazon.*

*For more details on our Metadata Guidelines, check out our Help Page:*

*If you have questions or believe you've received this email in error, please email us at kdp-quality-assurance@amazon.com*

*Best regards,*

*Amazon KDP*

As far as we could tell, the responsible party was not disciplined in any way despite many promises that this would not be permitted to happen again. As a result, the emboldened employee actually managed to get our entire KDP account terminated ten days after the seventh delisting, thereby removing our entire catalog of more than 100 digital editions by 35 authors from Amazon.

*Hello,*

*As last communicated in the message on January 21, 2019, we have identified the submission of content for which you did not have the necessary rights. Due to this and previous violations, we are terminating your account and your Agreement effective immediately.*

*As part of the termination process, we will close your KDP account and remove the books you have uploaded through our channels from sale on Amazon. Note that you are no longer eligible to receive unpaid royalties for sales that occurred prior to this termination.*

*Additionally, as per our Terms and Conditions, you are not permitted to open any new KDP accounts.*

*If you have any questions, please email us at kdp-account-status@amazon.com.*

*Regards,*

*Amazon.com*

Notice the way in which the nature of the supposed violation reported in the January 21st email is not the same violation cited in the January 31st email that terminated our KDP account. And then note the fact that none of these violations were even real in the first place! And finally, observe how the careless employee doesn't hesitate to put Amazon at serious legal risk from both us and the dozens of authors we publish by openly stating that Amazon would violate its contractual responsibility to pay us for books that we had already sold, and for which we were already owed royalties.

This unjustified action was clearly tortious interference in our separate legal agreements with our authors, which is probably why Amazon's legal department very quickly stepped in and restored our account after only 16 hours. We haven't had any problems with Amazon since, but at least one other publisher, a science fiction publishing house called Silver Empire, had its KDP account similarly shut down for no reason before it was restored.

While it is evident that Amazon's senior management doesn't harbor any serious desire to harass and drive away the various publishers, authors, and book buyers who use its bookselling services, it is equally apparent that they are not completely in control of their converged employees. And although, unlike Google, their decisions are not yet dictated by their internal extremists, the pattern of convergence growing within the organization is readily observable. And the convergence at Amazon is only going to get worse, as eventually one of the extremists will reach a sufficiently senior position to influence policy.

At that point, the virtual book burning will begin in earnest.

If establishment conservatives and libertarians who think the free market will solve everything seriously believe that we aren't heading rapidly towards a future where converged corporations won't hire people because they have read blacklisted books, watched unauthorized YouTube videos, or worn an article of disapproved clothing, they are as blind as the social justice activists in converged companies are to the inevitable consequences of their actions.

# Chapter 7
## Your Convergence Action Plan

The vast majority of people reading this book either work for, work with, use the services of, or buy products from, a converged company. In more than a few cases, people do all four.

Like an unfortunate individual diagnosed with cancer, when the inevitable consequences of convergence eventually strike you, you'll work through the stages of grief. Denial comes first, of course, but once you accept the reality of the situation, you'll progress to the bargaining stage. Often, it will go something like this. "Okay, so maybe my company is heavily converged and the writing is on the wall, but I like my job, my boss doesn't have it in for me, and maybe I can just keep my head down and keep my job. After all, sooner or later, the executives are bound to see that this direction is a mistake and they'll get rid of all the lunatics, right?"

Sadly, this does not often appear to be the case. The great weight of the observable evidence shows there is no easy way back from the brink for a heavily converged corporation. Since the social justice rot has already spread through the entire organization, simply firing the top executives will not cure anything. For example, Marvel Comics replaced Editor-in-Chief Axel Alonso with its Vice-President of International Development Brand Management, C.B. Cebulski, without any noticeable reduction in its commitment to social justice, the speed of its decline in unit sales, or the contempt even its lowest-level contract employees habitually display for Marvel's customers. In the aftermath of the repeated *Star Wars* movie disasters, Disney demoted Kathleen Kennedy and fired Rian Johnson, but brought Kevin Feige in to do for the *Star Wars* franchise what he has done for the Marvel Cinematic Universe.

In other words, the convergence continues apace. Damn the torpedoes, it's full speed ahead!

Convergence eventually spreads into every portion of an organization, from the top offices to the most hectic warehouse. Once you see that the bluehair brigade has even infested the loading dock, you can be assured that there is no coming back.

There is still a modicum of hope for moderately converged organizations. Such companies can beat convergence back, or at least freeze it in its track, but only if their unconverged management is strong enough to stand firm against the infiltrators in Marketing and HR. The Gillette division of Procter & Gamble launched a disastrous series of ads in 2019 that became notorious for taking aim at traditional masculine men who had already begun abandoning Gillette's razors in favor of growing beards. Other converged ad campaigns included televised commercials for women's razors predictably featuring morbidly obese and transsexual models. Fueled by the resultant loss of customers, Gillette took a massive $8 billion writedown. P&G executives can still straighten out its division, but will they do so or will they permit it to fall deeper into convergence? Only time will tell.

The odds of surviving convergence tend to be better in small companies. In fact, there is a recent example of a small company on the very brink of complete convergence that nevertheless managed to avoid that fate despite operating in a business sector you'd assume was doomed from the start.

The company is called Feminist Apparel, and it was founded by Alan Martofel, a male feminist, to market t-shirts to feminists and their male allies. It featured shirts displaying fierce feminist messages like "Don't tell me to smile" and "Misogyny Kills".

Like most self-described male feminists, Martofel had been guilty in the past of having had inappropriate sexual contact with his allies. He admitted in a social media post that he had behaved in a creepy manner, feeling up unsuspecting women on buses, at concerts, and when intoxicated at parties.

Martofel's nine female employees were quite rightly outraged by Martofel's admission, and demanded he step down from his own company. But, quite unexpectedly, Martofel salvaged the situation in a startling and unconventional way—he fired every single one of his employees. Now, if an admitted creep can save his career and his company with uncompromising action, it should be that much easier for good and decent people who have done nothing wrong to do the same. Unfortunately, due to corporate labor laws, such sweeping and rapid change can only be done by small businesses; in larger operations such actions will need to be done one department and division at a time.

But no matter what your relationship to a converged organization is, the first step when something happens to disrupt the ordinary course of business is always to stay calm and avoid taking any action while coolly assessing the situation. Don't quit, don't run crying to the media, and above all, do not apologize to anyone for anything! The worst thing you can do is to react emotionally and make rash decisions in a state of anger or panic; such decisions will almost always be suboptimal and against your own best interests.

The second step is to determine the exact state of your relationship with the converged organization, so you can sort out who is in the right and who is in the wrong, what your possible points of leverage are, who your potential allies might be, and what those allies might be able to do for you. Remember, corporate SJWs are so accustomed to easy victories that their reach very often exceeds their viable grasp. This means that the situation is seldom as hopeless as it looks when you first receive that weirdly fake-friendly email informing you that despite the fact that they are super good people who only wish the best for you, they can no longer permit you to earn money, buy things, or express your opinion.

Read their communications to you very carefully. In most cases, their justifications for their actions will be based on false and exaggerated mischaracterizations, if not outright lies. This doesn't necessarily mean that you'll be able to do anything to undo their actions, but it may point to a weakness in their case that you can exploit.

And even if you determine that there is simply nothing you can do to rectify things, you can still develop a plan to mitigate the damage and thereby avoid experiencing the soul-crushing defeat that those who hate and despise you so fervently wish you to feel. This, by the way, is why pleas for mercy and cries for sympathy are so counterproductive, as SJWs are sadists who actively boast about taking joy in the suffering of others.

Given the number of shirts and mugs being sold proclaiming "I drink male tears" or "I bathe in male tears", it should be obvious that throwing yourself on their mercy and appealing to their better nature is not going to be an effective response. They don't have a better nature, that's part of the problem in the first place.

Here are some thoughts on how you can deal with corporate convergence in five of the most common scenarios.

## You are a consumer who purchases material products from a converged corporation

This is both the most common situation in which we find ourselves today and the easiest with which to deal. If you spend your money on the products sold by a converged corporation, you are *directly* aiding and abetting the continued convergence of that organization, and because heavy convergence is usually reliant upon market dominance and a lack of competition, the convergence of the entire industry. You can rationalize this all you want by telling yourself that they have the best prices, they are the most convenient, or they are the industry standard, but don't fool yourself. By financially supporting them, you are part of the problem, not the solution.

In most cases, consumers buy products from a heavily converged company due to their brand loyalty to the pre-converged version of the company. But now that we all know how the quality and value provided by the brand will sooner or later go into a tailspin now that the inmates are running the converged asylum, so you can take solace in the certain knowledge that by abandoning them you won't be missing out on that perceived quality for long.

Consider how relieved the father who decided to give up the annual trip to Disneyland felt after reading about the complete disaster that was the Galaxy's Edge theme park launch. Or think about how glad the millions of former subscribers to ESPN feel after cutting the cord. They are missing out on nothing!

The process of abandoning a converged corporate ship as a consumer is straightforward. Identify alternative providers, determine which product or service best lines up with your needs, grit your teeth, and make the change. You may initially experience some pain in terms of price and service, but these are often temporary bumps. And besides, the pain is worth it. Just think of it as a personal sacrifice you are making to keep the lights on by fighting the further convergence of the West.

If you believe the organization is not fully converged, or if you are a long time customer whose business is important to it, you might want to take the time to contact the company and tell them why you are taking your business elsewhere. Such communication, especially in the form of an actual posted letter, can provide effective ammunition for the partisans fighting against convergence from within a company. Target operations executives such as regional managers, as they are not political animals and often have skin in the game based on the performance of their region.

One colleague pulled his considerable accounts from Bank of America after the company publicly declared that it would no longer offer financing to makers of "AR-style guns" in 2018 as part of a wave of corporate virtue-signaling against the Second Amendment. He wrote a letter to the regional manager explaining his decision to leave the bank after 20 years, and in response, the manager called him to explain he was hearing from many other customers with the same complaint and was using their complaints to fight the policy from the inside.

It may seem that companies frantically bend over backwards to fix criticism on social media, and that is a correct observation, but you must understand why. Social media accounts are run by junior members of the marketing department, already one of the first areas of a company to be infiltrated by SJWs. They live and die by the responses to the corporate social media accounts because they live or die based on the responses to their personal social media accounts. Outside of the marketing department, paper letters, emails, and phone calls to the middle managers and the executive office are much more powerful.

It's up to you to determine when it is time to stop buying goods and services from converged companies, but for the sake of the Good, the Beautiful, and the True, stop putting your money into the collection basket of the church of social justice!

## Your company buys or sells products from/to a converged company

A far less common situation is that the company you work for has a supply-based relationship with a converged company, either selling your products to them or vice-versa. Although you should still care about needlessly enriching the coffers of the converged, if you are in this category, your priority is a much more practical concern, which is the way that the negative effects of convergence will eventually have a negative effect on your own organization.

As revenues and profits fall for the heavily converged organization, they will increasingly lean on their suppliers to cut them better deals, desperate to make up for the shortfalls that are caused by their own incompetence. Elon Musk's Tesla, which suffered a 39% domestic sales drop in the third quarter of 2019, somehow managed to post a small profit for the quarter, which according to expert analysts who follow the industry was most likely based on the way it squeezed its battery supplier, Panasonic, for cost adjustments and rebates. As a supplier of a converged company, you should anticipate delayed payments, canceled orders, accounting hijinks, and eventually, a significant drop in your sales as convergence drives your corporate customer into the ground.

What about if you are on the other side of the transaction? If a converged company is your supplier, you had better be very wary and proactive about sourcing alternative providers. Product quality will eventually decline even as your prices are raised. Your relationship manager might be replaced with an incompetent diversity hire, while a rogue employee in the quality control department or accounting may decide that your business is no longer deemed desirable. In the blink of an eye, suppliers that had long been reliable can become a considerable detriment to your own organization, even a fatal one. And don't forget that unlike most cancers, convergence is communicable. It's entirely possible for the ads, the marketing programs, the packaging, and other propaganda from a converged supplier to infect your own organization!

If you are in charge, the solution to dealing with a converged supplier is easy. Direct your staff to find a new supplier and do the necessary work to build a relationship with them. But if you are not in charge, you have a lot more work ahead of you. You must be prepared to build a case against the existing supplier relationship to present to your superiors. But be careful. Only take this step if you are certain that your superiors are not themselves converged.

You will need to explain the concept of corporate cancer to them, which is best done by documenting material evidence of the negative effects of convergence at the supplier as well as some other examples from related industries that management will recognize. For reference, if you're dealing with an older superior, don't talk about Patreon and PayPal, they may have no clue who those companies are or believe that the examples are relevant in a very different industry. You will have to outline your expectations for the way in which continued negative effects are bound to have a material impact on your own organization.

Unfortunately, there is very little chance that your managers will initially be impressed by your concerns, at least not to the point of taking action. So, don't be dramatic or insistent, just make your case and let it go. The responsibility lies with them, not with you, and all you can do is provide them with the relevant information. The good news is that when the converged supplier inevitably begins slipping further, your superiors will recognize the problem much faster thanks to your efforts and will be sooner able to mitigate the damage. As an additional bonus, you will gain further trust within the organization, so don't hesitate to speak up and make your case when you see danger on the horizon.

## You are using the free services of a converged company

This is arguably the most precarious position in which anyone reading this book is likely to be. Remember, there is no such thing as a free lunch. If you are using the free services of Google, YouTube, Facebook, Twitter, LinkedIn, or any number of free online businesses, never forget that *you* are the product!

Furthermore, because you are using what amounts to a gift on the part of the converged company, you have neither leverage nor the protection of contract law. Since you're bringing nothing to the table, they can afford to discard you without risk. Even if you have built up a large following that you are able to monetize somehow, it is built on a foundation of sand that can collapse at any time. I had 33,000 Twitter followers when Twitter banned me in 2017; Milo Yiannopoulos had 338,000 when he was banned the year before. No one is too big to be deplatformed. Remember, a Twitter employee actually shut down President Trump's account in 2017.

And while the Twitter executives restored the suspended account just 11 minutes later, they probably won't rush to do so on behalf of someone who can't legally order a lethal drone strike on 1355 Market Street in San Francisco, no matter how many followers you have.

In my case, the Twitter deplatforming did not affect me in the slightest because Twitter was never the focus of my outreach to my audience, which primarily takes the form of my blog, my email lists, and my video channels. My monthly blog traffic actually grew five percent in the period immediately following the unexplained "suspension" of my Twitter account as people who had previously followed me there sought out my blog for the first time. I may be a small fish by Internet standards, but at least I am not subject to the control of the converged companies that police the free commons. The great N.N. Taleb rightly preaches the importance of personal antifragility in this unstable age, and it is better to have two thousand loyal supporters on an independent platform than two million on Facebook, Twitter, or any of the converged platforms where they can be vanished instantly with a single click.

This is not to say you should never utilize the free services that are available to you, only that you should never *rely* upon them. After all, Mao defeated the Kuomintang with 320,000 rifles, 9,000 machine guns and 900 artillery pieces captured from the Japanese. Don't hesitate to use the other side's weapons in a tactical manner when the opportunity presents itself, just don't base your operational strategy upon the false assumption that you will always have access to them.

## Your income relies upon the paid services of a converged company

On the one hand, your livelihood is in mortal danger even as you read these words. Social justice activists at the lowest levels of many major corporations have been given free reign to eliminate your income for even the slightest grievance, assuming they even bother to find an actual pretext for banning you instead of hiding behind an opaque code of conduct or a nebulous phrase in their terms of use.

Examples of people in this category include content creators using Patreon, Kickstarter, Indiegogo, or GoFundMe, YouTubers with monetized video channels, authors selling ebooks exclusively on Amazon, online businesses using PayPal and Stripe to provide their payment processing, and small businesses with a primary large customer like Dick's Sporting Goods.

If you are in this situation, your immediate goal should be to diversify every aspect of your business. If you only post videos on YouTube, then immediately begin to foster an audience on an unconverged platform like BitChute. If you bank with one of the major brands that has gotten into the censorship business by closing the accounts of conservatives, create your backup options now, even if you continue to bank with the bad guys for the time being. Local credit unions are an excellent option for this. As far as the payment processors and merchant services companies go, there are plenty of alternatives; you just might need to look outside the United States to find them.

The important thing is to be aware of the intrinsically unstable nature of the situation. A single news event, even a seemingly innocuous interview, can trigger a series of deplatformings that will catch you up in them. The activists at the big technology companies count on their market dominance and your naivety to give them the ability to shut you down in one fell swoop. By being flexible and establishing your backups before you are blacklisted, deplatformed, or demonetized, you can transform an attack on you into a growth opportunity instead of a operational disaster.

People like to support fighters. People love to back winners. Few things fire up a community of backers like seeing a targeted individual or organization take a shot from the big guys that is supposed to knock them down, only for them to bounce back immediately, stronger than before. We have backups, and in some cases, backups to our backups, in place for literally everything we do.

Furthermore, in this situation, the very act of deplatforming you is an increasingly risky one on the part of the converged platforms. Unlike the situation where you are using a platform for free, establishing an independent monetary relationship with fellow users of the platform, a relationship to which the platform is not privy and which in many cases its terms of use will specifically disavow, means that any action the platform takes to interfere with that relationship and harm either of the parties will make it potentially liable for any damages its action causes.

If that just made your ears perk up a little, your instincts are correct. But hold on to that thought, as we'll dive deeper into it in the following chapters.

Another thing to keep in mind is that even if a converged company on which you are dependent isn't targeting you, its actions can still be to your detriment. Amazon, for example, has destroyed the ebook market in which tens of thousands of self-published authors were making a good living by introducing Kindle Unlimited, which is eliminating an estimated $100 million in ebook sales per month. One of the reasons we were relaxed about being temporarily deplatformed by Amazon is that we had already set up online stores for both our print and ebook sales that now produce more revenue for us than Amazon or Audible did combined.

This book, for example, is available in ePub, Kindle, and MP4 formats at Arkhaven Comics, which is where we sell the ebooks and audiobooks directly, and is available in paperback from Castalia Direct.

It is always nerve-wracking for a content creator to depart the well-worn paths of success taken by previous creators and forge a brand new trail, but I guarantee it can be done. After all, this book is an example of the very scenario we are addressing here.

## You are employed by a converged company

At this point, if you are working at a company that is converged to some degree, you have a pretty good idea of the challenges that face you. You may have even picked up this book in the first place after observing the signs of convergence developing around you. In either case, staying cool is always going to be your first priority. As you know, you are caught between the mythical Scylla and Charybdis, if both monsters from *The Odyssey* were humorless social justice activists.

On the one hand, the converged HR department will sooner or later come gunning for you for one reason or another. Just by being yourself, you will set off their radar, unless you are extraordinarily clever at blending in with the lunatic fringe. Once you are identified as a crimethinker, or are suspected of being a white male, or show any signs of having voted for President Trump, the activists will relentlessly stalk you and attempt to get you fired. The great Google witch hunt of November 2016 is the primary example of this, but remember that it occurs in some form in every single organization in which social justice warriors gain sufficient power.

And don't think you're safe if you have the privilege to be a woman or a minority. In fact, the converged usually go after women and minorities who fail to adhere to the social justice narrative in an even more vicious manner than they do white men, because they are viewed as traitors as well as being haters. Don't forget that as far as the converged are concerned, Asian men are not minorities, they are honorary Aryans, which is practically the same thing as being a Nazi who merits punching on sight.

On the other hand, even if the converged employees don't manage to hound you out of a job, the probabilities are very high, to the point of near certainty, that their actions are going to lead to layoffs, rightsizing, pay cuts, the revision of compensation plans, the suspension of bonuses, and other forms of corporate mayhem. Even if you manage to evade the disemployment pogrom, will your job be worth keeping? You'll likely be expected to work more for less pay as the value of the company's name on your resume declines in line with its sales. Perhaps the most damaging thing in the long run is the company's appearance in a long series of dismal news stories, as fair or not, the converged company's performance will reflect on the way you are perceived by future employers.

Think about how you thought about a Googler five years ago. You probably pictured a really smart guy who graduated near the top of his class from a prestigious university. And how do you imagine the average Googler now? A goony soy boy, an angry, blue-haired trans-woman, or an affirmative action diversity hire, right?

While you have a few options, none of them involve staying with your current employer in the long term. If the company is heavily converged, there will be no turning back. There is no fixing it; it just doesn't happen. So forget any hopes you may have entertained that things will just work out somehow and start developing your plan to move onward and upward.

Your best place to start, and something you should be doing re-gardless of whether your company is already converged or not, is a combination of internal and external networking. Find the fellow travelers in your company who also see the writing in the wall. Talk to them about the problems you all know the organization is facing in the near future. Many of them will be perceptive enough to see there are problems, but they may not have the knowledge or the vocabulary to fully grasp the situation. For example, many older people understand that there are freaks working in the office, but they don't know what a social justice warrior actually is. Explaining some of the basic concepts in this book to them is a good place to start.

These coworkers will be an excellent source of referrals to jobs and have other ideas and suggestions on how to best get out of your predica-ment. At the same time, you should be externally networking with former classmates, colleagues from other companies, and anyone else you've known in your school or professional career. The best way to get a job is to hear about it from someone you know.

You should also create an inventory of your skills and knowledge, then create a list of companies whose needs are in line with your skills. Remember, as your converged employer falters, its non-converged rivals will surge. Jumping ship to a healthier competitor is an excellent move for any competent employee. There are other ways to profit from convergence as well. One diabolically clever friend of mine has made a fortune shorting the stocks of converged companies and investing in the stocks of their publicly-traded and less-converged rivals.

But while you're working on your exit plan, keep your mouth shut and don't rock the sinking ship. Expressing any discontent will bring swift retribution down upon you. James Damore had no idea that simply pointing out the obvious about Google's lack of intellectual diversity would result in his disemployment. He mistakenly believed the company's own stated code of conduct and HR rules would protect him. That was exceedingly naive!

Once you've secured your next position, then you can safely let them know your opinion on the way out, but always remember that no one can fix a fully-converged company. Not the CEO, not the Board of Directors, and certainly not you.

## Conclusion

American companies have opened themselves to the corporate cancer of convergence with alarming enthusiasm. Large, market-dominating companies have turned against their customers, their employees, and every principle of good business in pursuit of social justice virtue-signaling. Despite all the well-documented failures of this strategy in the marketplace, this phenomenon shows no signs of slowing down.

Not yet, anyhow.

In the meantime, the best thing you can do for yourself and for your organization is to spot the signs of convergence early and stop its spread. Just be aware that in many organizations, it is far too late, the cancer has already metastasized and spread to all departments, all divisions, and is eating away at the entire organization from the inside out.

Regardless of your relationship with corporate America, never forget that you, and only you, can be responsible for yourself, your income, and your career. Once you've identified a converged entity, you can either ride the dragon for as long as the ride lasts, or you can do your best to kill the monster. The question is: are you ready, willing, and able to take on corporate cancer with all the ruthlessness and determination that is required to beat it? Because I assure you, it can be done.

# Chapter 8

## Case Study:
## The Road to a Deplatforming

In August 2018, I decided to create a new comic book series. All the rumors of a blackwashed or sex-swapped James Bond floating around, combined with the dark and disturbing conspiracy theories revolving around Pizzagate, Jeffrey Epstein's island, and the incredible political phenomenon of Q, made me think that there was a real opportunity to invent a new action hero for the 21st Century. I enlisted the formidable creative powers of The Legend Chuck Dixon, the longtime writer of *Batman*, *The Punisher*, and many other comic series published by DC and Marvel Comics, and together we came up with a concept that inserted a political action thriller into Arkhaven's existing superhero world.

We named this concept *Alt-Hero:Q*, selected a first-rate pair of artists to illustrate it, and created a campaign for it on a crowdfunding platform called Indiegogo. We chose Indiegogo over Kickstarter for two reasons. First, Kickstarter was known to be somewhat converged and occasionally given to deplatforming campaigns and creators of which SJWs did not approve. Second, Indiegogo was already home to a number of independent comic campaigns, chief among them the very successful *Cyberfrog* campaign by ex-DC illustrator Ethan Van Sciver.

The campaign went smoothly and was completely successful. In 30 days, we raised $103,267 from 1,456 backers. This was sufficient to more than cover the cost of producing six 24-page issues as well as paperback and omnibus collections of all six issues. While the outcome wasn't quite as spectacular as the $244,835 we'd raised for the original *Alt-Hero* series on a different crowdfunding platform, much less the $538,456 Ethan Van Sciver had raised for *Cyberfrog: Bloodhoney* on Indiegogo, on a per-issue basis it was actually more successful than our previous effort.

On September 26, Indiegogo sent us an email informing us that they would be sending us the $96,000 we were owed, which was the total amount raised less their platform and payment processing fees. We promptly set to work with The Legend and the artists, eager to see what could be done with what was without question the best team we'd yet managed to assemble.

But not everyone was pleased with our success. One woman, a self-styled *Rolling Stone* reporter named Amanda Robb, seemed to be dead set on attempting to hinder us in some way. In fact, a few days before the end of the *Alt-Hero:Q* campaign, she released an investigative report on National Public Radio in cooperation with Al Letson of The Center for Investigative Reporting's Reveal entitled "Never meet your (super) heroes".

The report was a shameless hit piece. Robb had been stalking me, everyone associated with me, and more than a few people who were only casually acquainted with me for months. And she was very unhappy with everyone's complete refusal to speak with her on or off the record, most notably with Pax Dickinson, whose epic runaround of her can be read in "Appendix A: In Which I Express A Heartfelt Apology To *Rolling Stone* Journalist Amanda Robb", and now represents the platinum standard in media relations as far as I am concerned.

The investigative report was intended as red meat—or perhaps I should say, pure vegan soy—for white liberals terrified by the Alt-Right bogeyman, and purported to inform them of the latest right-wing hate-assault on tolerance, equality, diversity, inclusivity, and progress. It also featured a gotcha interview with Chuck Dixon, of whom Al Letson claimed, rather dubiously, to have been a long-time fan.

> *There's a new battlefield in the culture wars: comic books. The alt-right now has gotten in the business, led by a buxom, Confederate flag-waving superhero named Rebel and a white vigilante who turns immigrants over to ICE.*

The primary focus of the hit piece was to suggest that we had somehow engaged in illicit fundraising or money laundering, which in light of the way Arkhaven produced and shipped tens of thousands of comics funded by the original *Alt-Hero* campaign, demonstrated an impressive lack of understanding of the way money laundering actually works. They also failed to note that while the total amount raised was impressive, there were also 2,190 backers, which meant that the average donation was $111.79, higher than the average crowdfunding project, but neither suspiciously nor spectacularly so.

Nor, for that matter, did I create, own, fund, or have anything to do with the Freestartr site. And finally, Superhero Graphic Novels is not exactly "a pretty small category" on Amazon. The category happens to contain more than a few titles you might recognize, such as *Superman, Batman, Amazing Spider-Man, Flash, X-Men: The Dark Phoenix Saga,* and so on. While it was certainly unusual for a new superhero comic from an upstart comics publisher to outsell all of these well-known standbys and hit number one, however briefly, this was just another indication of the unexpectedly strong support for the project, not the result of any Machiavellian manipulations on our part.

> *Al Letson: So Vox Day claims to have gotten money to produce these comic books through a crowdfunding website. I'm on that site and it says he started off trying to raise $25,000, but he raised close to $236,000. That just amazes me.*
>
> *Amanda Robb: It's actually pretty unbelievable.*

*Al Letson:* Where is that money coming from?

*Amanda Robb:* Well that's the $236,000 question. It's very hard to tell. Most of it's from anonymous donors and a lot of it comes in very large increments, some up to $5,000 each which is weird because the average donation to a crowdfunding project is about $66.

*Al Letson:* But we don't know if he actually raised that money. It looks like it, but we don't know that for a fact.

*Amanda Robb:* I think that's a really good point, because Alt-Hero was raising money on a crowdfunding site called FreeStartr, and apparently Vox Day helped create it. It's a private site. It's totally black box. There's no way to find out who made most of the donations, where the money came from, where it went, if it actually existed. I did find out that the company that processed the credit card payments decided to stop working with FreeStartr a few months back, and I tried to get in touch with the company to find out why and they wouldn't talk to me. Then Alt-Hero had already way surpassed its fundraising goal and is publishing now a series of comic books.

*Al Letson:* So who's distributing Alt-Hero?

*Amanda Robb:* Amazon.

*Al Letson:* Why is Amazon distributing this book?

*Amanda Robb:* Well, I asked Amazon, and someone from their PR department got back to me. He said it falls within their guidelines. He helpfully sent me a link to their guidelines so I click on them and it says their definition of offensive material is, and I'm quoting, "What we deem offensive is probably about what you would expect."

*Al Letson:* That doesn't make sense, because I find this offensive and they don't find it offensive.

*Amanda Robb:* Well it's a very movable goalpost, it turns out. Amazon changes what it thinks is offensive all the time.

*Al Letson:* I don't know. That rule seems pretty flimsy.

*Amanda Robb:* Not only is Amazon distributing the digital version, it's number one in its category on Amazon.

*Al Letson:* So how does this book become a bestseller?

*Amanda Robb:* Well, it's possible that a lot of people are really reading it, and it's possible that Vox is taking advantage of something that Amazon does which is called micro-categorizing. So right now, one of the issues of Alt-Hero is the number one new release in Superhero Graphic Novels. That's a pretty small category, but it is number one in that category.

*Al Letson:* Amanda Robb at the Investigative Fund is here to tell us what happened since "Alt-Hero" launched back in the spring. Amanda, what are Chuck Dixon and Vox Day up to now?

*Amanda Robb:* Well, they're still working on "Alt-Hero." They're on their fourth issue right now. They're both crowdfunding for new comic books on Indiegogo. Vox's comic, which Chuck is writing with him, is another "Alt-Hero." It's about QAnon. Q is sort of the conspiracy theory about pedophile Democrats and Trump's secret plans to defeat the globalist [sic]. They raised $62,000 in the first week.

What I didn't know at the time the NPR piece ran is that three weeks before it was broadcast, Amanda Robb contacted Indiegogo and attempted to interfere with the *Alt-Hero:Q* campaign by casting aspersions on the authenticity of our fundraising. And while she was no more successful with Indiegogo than she had been with Amazon, some seeds of doubt about the campaign's legitimacy were apparently planted.

Still, the campaign was successful, and two weeks after the crowdfunding was over, a news site dedicated to the comics industry, *Bleeding Cool*, published an extensive interview with me. The interviewer was the founder and Editor-in-Chief of the site. At 17,000 words, the interview entitled "Vox Day: Altered States of America" was ludicrously long, but because it declared many of the spurious accusations that had been made about me were false and asserted that I had "earned a place at the table" of the comics establishment, it enraged the SJWs in the comics industry.

While the reaction on Twitter and other social media was relatively muted, behind the scenes there was pure fury and outrage. Employees threatened to quit, industry professionals threatened a lack of future cooperation with the site, and some advertisers even threatened to pull their advertising if the interview was not recanted immediately. As I had warned the editor *in the interview itself,* the industry SJWs could not be accommodated or reasoned with, and indeed, they were out for his head.

It did not take them long to obtain it. Early in the morning the very next day, his successor posted a public apology for the crimethink he had committed by interviewing me.

### *An Apology Concerning Vox Day: We Made a Mistake*

*We at Bleeding Cool wish to issue an apology.*

*Bleeding Cool does not support bigotry of any kind, nor will we become a bullhorn for the bigots of the world to go off.*

*Today one of our writers made an error in judgment resulting in giving exposure to viewpoints that we abhor. We will do better, going forward, and that is a promise. The author admits that this was an extreme error of judgment that never should have been made and that other members of the Bleeding Cool writing staff were unaware of the contents of this article.*

*In a first step towards that end we are announcing, effective immediately, I am stepping into the role of Editor-in-Chief and will be implementing new review policies across the Bleeding Cool teams.*

*Yesterday an extensive interview was run with publisher, author, and political figure Vox Day.*

*The intention of the interview was to investigate Day's political and ideological views, and his operations as a publisher. But these intentions do not matter. The intent of the article and interview were poorly executed, and poorly communicated.*

*While the intentions of the author might have been one thing, the reality of the situation is another. Bleeding Cool would like to issue a sincere apology to everyone for the article in question.*

*We do not, in any way, agree with the ideology of Vox Day. We do not support divisiveness in the fan community, or in our culture at large. We do not support those that try to bring down others. We support diversity in all aspects of pop culture. We support everyone fighting the good fight against bigotry and only wish we could play a part in making not only the internet but the world a safer place for all individuals. We cannot apologize enough for the people we have offended. We cannot apologize enough for the breach of trust this has had with our readers and people within the community. We hope you'll be willing to give us a chance to win back that trust in some capacity.*

*We will do better.*

Perhaps the most amusing thing about the whole situation was that nothing could have underlined the points I made in the interview about the convergence of the comics industry more clearly than the decision of the Bleeding Cool editors to disappear the interview and demote its author. But while I couldn't have cared less about the fate of the interview or the interviewer, some of the other fallout from the kerfuffle was rather less funny and considerably more troublesome.

This was because the SJW outrage generated by the interview was not only directed at Bleeding Cool. It was also aimed at Indiegogo, which crumbled under the pressure almost as quickly as the comic site's leadership did. Despite having previously declared that there were no issues with the campaign while it was running, after receiving many complaints in response to the publication of the interview, the decision to take down Arkhaven's *Alt-Hero:Q* campaign was made, and made almost instantly. In fact, Indiegogo's decision was made so quickly that the campaign was taken down before Bleeding Cool managed to take the interview down.

However, there was a serious problem with Indiegogo's remarkably rapid response to the external SJW pressure. *The crowdfunding campaign had come to an end two weeks before.* What's more, after the conclusion of the campaign on September 26, Indiegogo informed Arkhaven that it would pay the $94,096 representing the net amount owed for the campaign "on or about September 28, 2018." But that payment could no longer be made, because in addition to retroactively taking down the completed campaign in response to the interview, Indiegogo had also decided to immediately refund all of the money received from campaign's backers.

All 1,456 contributors to the *Alt-Hero:Q* campaign received the same email.

### Your transaction has been refunded

*Your transaction to ALT-HERO:Q on Indiegogo has been refunded!*

*Indiegogo's Trust and Safety Team determined this campaign didn't comply with our Terms of Use. You'll no longer receive any perks associated with this transaction. Please visit our help center for further information on how Indiegogo protects users.*

At first, I was not alarmed when news of the campaign refunds began to trickle in from our backers. I initially thought it must be a tremendous mistake on Indiegogo's part, because I was under the impression that the money they were refunding to our backers had already been paid to us as promised. But, as we soon discovered, the scheduled payment hadn't taken place, and moreover, Indiegogo had very publicly posted a banner on the campaign page that falsely claimed we had somehow violated their terms of use after the fact.

*This campaign has been closed by Trust and Safety due to a violation of our Terms of Use. The campaign will no longer be accepting contributions, and the Campaign Owners no longer have access to the campaign.*

Complicating matters was the email that Indiegogo sent us ten hours after making the decision to take down the campaign, which we received after we'd already been hearing that various backers had been refunded the full amount of their contributions.

### Your Account is Currently Frozen

*Hello Arkhaven,*

*Unfortunately, due to unusual activity, we have frozen your Indiegogo account. No contributions or campaign disbursements can be processed for your account at this time.*

*There are a variety of reasons that this might have happened, and it's possible that our team just needs a little more information to verify your identity.*

*Please respond to this email within 48 hours and we can help resolve the issue. Thank you for your cooperation, and we look forward to hearing from you.*

*Sincerely,*

*The Indiegogo Team*

Naturally, we inquired as to what this unusual activity might be, what we needed to do in order to unfreeze our account, and why our backers were receiving notices of refunds. But the next day, we received the following email.

*Thank you for your patience. We appreciate your cooperation throughout the review process. Unfortunately, after reviewing your campaign and campaign activity, we have determined that your campaign, "ALT-HERO:Q," is too risky to continue raising funds through Indiegogo. At this time, we have removed your campaign from our platform and will be processing refunds for your campaign.*

*Indiegogo strives to maintain a balance between being an equal opportunity platform while simultaneously protecting the security of our users, and the decision to remove your campaign was not made lightly. We appreciate your understanding and sincerely apologize for any inconvenience.*

The review process? What review process? We still didn't know what "unusual activity" or "too risky" meant, nor did we understand how Indiegogo could start processing refunds that apparently had already been refunded to the backers. And if the decision to remove our campaign "was not made lightly", why had it been taken so quickly and without even talking to us? The timeline of events simply didn't make any sense when viewed from our perspective at the time, and in retrospect, clearly indicated the real reason for the cancellation of the campaign:

| | |
|---|---|
| Oct 11, 1:10 a.m. | Bleeding Cool interview published. |
| Oct 11, 2:10 a.m. | Indiegogo sends ACCOUNT CURRENTLY FROZEN email. |
| Oct 11, 2:18 a.m. | Indiegogo sends refund emails to backers. |
| Oct 12, 4:40 a.m. | Bleeding Cool interview taken down. |
| Oct 12, 11:11 a.m. | Indiegogo sends CAMPAIGN REMOVED email. |
| Oct 13, 11:00 a.m. | Bleeding Cool posts apology and announces new Managing Editor. |

As news of the *ex post facto* campaign cancellation spread, SJWs celebrated while independent comics producers expressed not-unreasonable fear about the possibility that their ongoing crowdfunding campaigns would be the next one targeted for being taken down. Ethan Van Sciver and other Comicsgate creators openly speculated about the reasons for the cancellation, but were comforted by Indiegogo's assurances that the *Alt-Hero:Q* campaign was a special case that did not herald additional deplatformings, assurances which turned out to be largely, though not completely, true. While Indiegogo left *Cyberfrog: Bloodhoney* and most other independent comic campaigns untouched, it did cancel a campaign by a small independent comics creator called Electric Dinosaur as well as one by a torrent-based alternative to YouTube called BitChute in the months following the *Alt-Hero:Q* campaign's cancellation.

Despite all of the confusion and rumors flying around that incorrectly blamed everything from anti-semitism to money laundering to white supremacy for the cancellation of the campaign, it was perfectly clear to us from the start that Indiegogo's action was little more than an overreaction to the SJW outrage over the Bleeding Cool article. Nor were we alone in reaching the obvious conclusion, as the title of Mike Glyer's piece at the science fiction history site File 770 demonstrates: "After Bleeding Cool Interviews Vox Day, IndieGoGo Axes Latest Alt-Hero Comic Campaign."

*Post hoc ergo propter hoc* notwithstanding, that indeed turned out to be the case.

But neither Indiegogo's reasons nor motivations were our concern at the time. We had more practical matters that required addressing. Once we realized that Indiegogo had not paid us and was not responding to our emailed inquiries, we immediately began to prepare for what we knew was likely to be a long and tedious legal dispute. Fortunately, neither deplatforming nor legal conflict were new to me, as I had been previously deplatformed for crimethink by SFWA, Twitter, and GoodReads, and, as the head of a computer game development house, endured a two-year legal battle with our publisher, the now-defunct GT Interactive, a battle that began with GT refusing to send us a simple letter and concluded with them writing us a check for nearly a quarter million dollars.

Our first concern was to keep the level of our supporters' morale high by demonstrating that this deplatforming could not prevent us from publishing *Alt-Hero:Q.* While we waited in vain for a response from Indiegogo's support department during the 30 days set forth by their terms of use, we contacted a number of crowdfunding sites in order to set up a replacement campaign for our outraged backers, many of whom were publicly vowing to double, or even triple, their previous contributions.

> **Initial Dispute Resolution:** *Most disputes can be resolved without resort to litigation. Except for intellectual property and small claims court claims, the parties agree to use their best efforts to settle any dispute, claim, question, or disagreement directly through consultation with the Indiegogo support department support@indiegogo.com and good faith negotiations shall be a condition to either party initiating a lawsuit or arbitration.*

> **Binding Arbitration:** *If the parties do not reach an agreed-upon solution within a period of thirty (30) days from the time informal dispute resolution is initiated under the Initial Dispute Resolution provision above, then either party may initiate binding arbitration as the sole means to resolve claims, subject to the terms set forth below.*

Finding a replacement turned out to be a little more difficult than we expected, because two of the first crowdfunding sites we contacted turned us down without giving us any reason for doing so. As we later learned, at least one of them had gotten in touch with Indiegogo immediately after we contacted them and were informed by Indiegogo that the reason for the cancellation was an unspecified violation of their terms of use. But we did eventually find a crowdfunding site that was willing to host our 2.0 campaign, and the backers demonstrated their commitment to the cause by providing us with $134,428.88, a 42.9 percent increase over the amount we'd originally raised.

This was important, because it not only boosted everyone's morale and allowed us to proceed with producing the *Alt-Hero:Q* comics, but provided us with a small war chest to begin the legal dispute. In addition, we already had an informal legal team known collectively as the Legal Legion of Evil, a collection of lawyers, law students, and paralegals from around the world who are willing to work in coordination on an *ad hoc, pro bono* basis. In law, jurisdiction matters, which normally would have prevented those licensed to practice in other states and countries from getting directly involved, but in this case, there were lawyers who were backers of the original campaign and therefore possessed legal standing to take action on their own behalf.

The core legal team was chosen and quickly set to work analyzing the Indiegogo terms of use, beginning with the Legal Disputes Subject to Arbitration, Dispute Resolution, and Class Action Waiver section. The terms specified the use of the JAMS arbitration system and the JAMS Streamlined Arbitration Rules and Procedures, none of which were familiar to any of us, so we immediately began studying both the terms and the Streamlined Rules and Procedures with all the intensity of a dying sinner in fear of imminent hellfire engaged in Biblical exegesis.

The first thing we noted was that Indiegogo had obviously interfered in what their terms established as agreements between us and our backers, separate agreements to which Indiegogo was not a part. Second, whoever had written their terms had an imperfect grasp of the English language.

### 3. CREATING AND RUNNING A CAMPAIGN

*When you, as a Campaign Owner creates [sic] a Campaign on the Site and asks [sic] for Contributions, you understand that you are entering into separate legal agreements with both Indiegogo and with Contributors, and the following rules apply (in addition to the all other [sic] Terms and Additional Policies).*

This told us four very important things about the situation. First, by refunding our backers without our approval, Indiegogo appeared to have engaged in tortious interference in the separate legal agreements between those backers and us. Second, this apparent interference suggested that our backers would have standing to get involved in the dispute, although they would have to pay $250 apiece to do so. Third, the grammatical infelicities suggested that we were not dealing with first-rate legal minds here, and fourth, the speed of their initial response combined with their vague communications and the incorrectly-worded terms of use strongly suggested that whatever the reason for the deplatforming might have actually been, it had not been carefully constructed upon a sound legal foundation.

The second thing upon which we focused ultimately turned out to be a red herring, even though it was more damaging to us than we had any reason to know at the time. We thought the combination of the false public claims that we had violated Indiegogo's terms of use, combined with the obvious implications of "unusual activity" and "too risky", amounted to defamation, particularly in light of the rumors of money laundering that we'd heard were circulating through the comics industry. We even felt that we had caught them red-handed on the basis of two statements released by industry professionals, but that turned out not to be the case for reasons that will eventually be addressed in the next chapter.

And the third thing we noted was that according to the terms of use, the money we had been expecting to receive on or about September 28 was quite literally our money. By rights it belonged to us, not to Indiegogo, and therefore they had no right to refund it to the backers. Second, by failing to deliver our money to us, Indiegogo appeared to have spectacularly failed in its self-appointed fiduciary duty to us as our limited agent.

*l.*   *Service Fees. Campaign Owners are charged a Service Fee as a portion of the Contributions they raise (the "Service Fees"). The Service Fees are effective on the date that the Service Fees are posted, and may be updated from time to time. Service Fees will be charged at the then-current rate. In connection receiving [sic] Contributions from Contributors, Campaign Owners appoint Indiegogo as the*

*Campaign Owner's limited agent for the sole purpose of receiving, holding, and settling payments to such Campaign Owner. As a Campaign Owner's agent, Indiegogo's receipt of Contributions on a Campaign Owner's behalf is the same as receipt of Contributions by directly by a Campaign Owner.*

These three elements were the foundation of our legal case, about which more in the next chapter on the arbitration itself. The battle lines had been drawn. Our initial legal salvo had been launched and while it was one that Indiegogo did not see coming, with $56.5 million from five rounds of investment, big-name investors like Richard Branson, Draper Associates, and Institutional Venture Partners, and one of Silicon Valley's best and most renowned law firms on their side, it looked as if we had rather an uphill battle in front of us.

Although the morale of our backers was extremely high and we knew that scores, if not hundreds, of our backers were prepared to either take legal action independently or join a group action, I was skeptical that we had enough collective firepower to do any serious damage to such a well-funded corporation. At the same time, I knew we couldn't simply accept the situation like so many others had before, because that would only lead to more innocent creators being victimized by a now-weaponized bureaucracy. On January 3, 2019, we filed for arbitration as per the Indiegogo Terms of Use effective May 25, 2018.

All we really believed to be possible at that point was to get back some of the money we were originally owed, and perhaps get our account restored so we could go about our business of producing bestselling comic books that shatter the current cultural narrative.

As it happens, I could not have been more wrong.

# Chapter 9

## Indiegogo Case Study: The Arbitration Process and Outcome

*[REDACTED UNTIL OCTOBER 11, 2021]*

*The parties to the arbitrations have come to a resolution on the matter. The arbitrations have been terminated. We will not be making any further statement about it. Please do not ask questions or probe for details about the resolution of the matter.*

**ITEM**: On April 9, 2019, the digital edition of *Alt-Hero:Q #1 Where We Go One* was released on Amazon. It swiftly rose to become the #1 New Release in the Superhero Graphic Novel category, surpassing, most notably, *The Batman Who Laughs #4* and *Superman #10*.

**ITEM**: *Alt-Hero:Q #2 Not Dead Enough* was released on October 26, 2019. Like its predecessor, it became an Amazon category bestseller.

# Chapter 10

## Case Study:
## A Patreon Deplatforming

Owen Benjamin is a comedian, a farmer of goats, and a mainstay of Unauthorized.TV. A self-admitted height supremacist—at 6'8" he is a literal giant—he utilizes music and irreverence to equal effect in his comedy. Not only has he had the unexpected honor of having a joke stolen by David Chappelle, he *actually told it better* than Netflix's 20-million-dollar man.

Seriously.

Once a rising figure in Hollywood, where he appeared in movies such as *House Bunny* with Anna Faris and Emma Stone, hosted the Art Directors Guild's awards, and dated actress Christina Ricci, Owen was banished from the entertainment industry and blacklisted for bad-think after publicly opposing the child abuse inherent in underage sex change hormone regimes. As a result, he was fired by his agent at CAA, fired by his manager, attacked by former friends, and disavowed by former colleagues.

Even worse, venues in which he had previously performed, even those which he had successfully sold out, now refused to let him perform in them. He was kicked off Twitter, demonetized by Google, and on October 9, 2019, he was informed that his Patreon account had been terminated by Patreon Trust & Safety.

His relations with Patreon hadn't always been difficult. After first creating his account on November 8, 2016, his number of backers, or "patrons" as they are known in Patreon-speak, had grown steadily. By March 2018, he was bringing in $8,739.44 per month from 1,353 patrons.

> *From: Patreon*
>
> *Date: Thu, Apr 5, 2018 at 1:57 PM*
>
> *Subject: $8,739.44 was just sent to you from Patreon!*
>
> *To: Owen Benjamin*
>
> *Woohoo - you just got paid!*
>
> *$8,739.44 was just sent out to you from Patreon covering earnings up to April 5, 2018. You will notice that $8,739.44 has been deducted from your pending earnings to reflect this payment. You can view your account here.*
>
> *Congrats again and thank you from all of us at Patreon.*

Everything appeared to be going swimmingly. After 16 months of successful collaboration and continued growth, there was no indication whatsoever that Patreon had any problems with him. But less than two weeks later, on April 16, Owen was informed by PayPal that he had been permanently demonetized by the money-transfer giant due to what PayPal claimed, without any explanation or substantiation, was his "violation of PayPal's Acceptable Use Policy".

> *Dear Owen,*
>
> *After a recent review of your account activity, it has been determined that you are in violation of PayPal's Acceptable Use Policy. Therefore, your account has been permanently limited.*
>
> *Please remove all references to PayPal from your website/s and/or auction/s. This includes not only removing PayPal as a payment option, but also the PayPal logo and PayPal shopping cart.*

*You may withdraw the funds on your PayPal account balance to your registered bank account. Information on how to withdraw funds from your PayPal Account can be found at our Help Centre.*

*Customers who are permanently limited for violating the Acceptable Use Policy are not permitted to use PayPal services and are not permitted to open new or additional PayPal accounts.*

*You can find the complete PayPal Acceptable Use Policy by clicking Legal at the bottom of any PayPal page.*

*Sincerely,*

*Paul*

*PayPal, Brand Risk Management*

This action on the part of PayPal not only made it harder for his fans to support him directly, but also had a second-order effect of removing one method for them to support him on Patreon as well. The day after PayPal notified him that they were taking down his account, Owen received the following email from Patreon.

*Sidney (Patreon)*

*Apr 17, 6:23 PM PDT*

*Hey Owen,*

*My name is Sidney and I'm on Patreon's Trust & Safety team. We have been notified by PayPal that we must disable PayPal as a payment method offered on your account.*

*PayPal has a stricter set of rules and regulations than Patreon and they reserve the right to not offer their services to accounts of their choosing. This is in line with their terms of service which means it's something with which we must comply.*

*You may still process payments using credit cards as we work to onboard new payment partners.*

*Let me know if you have any other questions or concerns.*

*All the best,*

*Patreon Trust and Safety Monday-Friday*

This was a problem too, though not a particularly serious one. Most people who use PayPal have credit cards as well, and have no problem switching from one form of online payment to the other. But it was a harbinger of bigger problems soon to come. Very soon, as it turned out.

One thing we have learned over time is how much quiet inter-company communication there is among the SJWs working in the media-technology complex. There is an incredible amount of job-hopping from one converged company to another; particularly in the budding field of Compliance and Trust and Safety. And not all of the communication that is taking place between companies is comprised of direct emails and telephone calls.

As I described in *SJWs Always Lie*, SJWs are very sensitive to even the most minute adjustments in the current narrative, to which they tend to react in uniform like a school of fish. This means that once one converged organization publicly identifies an individual as a target for deplatforming, other organizations are often quick to follow suit.

That is why, having received the signal from PayPal that the co-median was guilty of crimethink, Patreon's Trust and Safety team immediately leaped into action, scouring not only its own platform but also Twitter, Facebook, YouTube, and other social media platforms for any evidence that would provide an excuse for it to take similar action against him. It didn't take them long to find it, because just one day later, Owen received the following email from an unnamed member of Trust and Safety.

*Patreon TnS team (Patreon)*

*Apr 18, 11:01 AM PDT*

*Hi Owen,*

*I work for Patreon's Trust and Safety team and I am contacting you because you have violated Patreon's community guidelines.*

*Patreon values the important work comedians do and has no interest in devolving your or any other comedian's expression to conformity. We understand that comedians push the boundaries and that as a company we hold immense power over the creators on our platform. We don't want to create an environment of fear for comedians that they will lose their primary source of income because of one bad joke. But Patreon also must maintain a community where people from various backgrounds and experiences feel safe on the platform.*

*Tweets you've published (and that have since been removed from Twitter) perpetuate negative stereotypes concerning protected classes. I'm specifically referencing your tweet concerning black people and AIDS. Your recent Facebook post and live-streams about Hollywood and rape survivors also violate our guidelines. Patreon does not allow shaming private or public survivors of sexual assault. I understand you are aiming for shock value in your work. Whether or not shock value is the sole intent, Patreon draws the line at content containing hateful rhetoric and harassing sexual assault victims.*

*You may consider this as censorship, and be tempted to continue to act as a provocateur in defense of freedom of speech. I want to remind you that freedom of speech allows a platform such as Patreon to create a community with our own guidelines. These guidelines are designed to ensure that creators of all types can use Patreon effectively to build their creative businesses. If you choose to violate our guidelines again your page will be removed.*

*Let us know if you have any questions.*

*Kindest regards,*

*Patreon Trust and Safety Monday-Friday*

With this shot across the bow, Trust and Safety revealed that its baleful eye was now firmly fixed upon the comedian, and that it would henceforth be actively monitoring tweets on Twitter, posts on Facebook, videos on YouTube, and any other online activity it could find. Believe it or not, Patreon actually claims the right to police the behavior of its many creators, not just on Patreon's own site, but across the Internet and even in one's private life. It even asserts this right in its Terms of Use.

*Abusive conduct*

*TLDR: Be responsible and don't violate our policies.*

*You are responsible for all activity on your account. If you violate our policies we may terminate your account.*

*Don't do anything illegal, abusive towards others, or that abuses our site in a technical way. If you are a creator raising funds on Patreon, we may be held accountable for what you do with those funds. As a result, we also look at what you do with your membership off our platform.*

Now, it is hardly surprising that a comedian, especially a relatively young and popular one, will occasionally say things that someone, somewhere, would find offensive. The societal role of the comedian is in the tradition of the King's Fool, the one man in the kingdom who was permitted to say the things that are not customarily said. From Lenny Bruce to Richard Pryor and David Chappelle, comedians have been lauded specifically for their willingness to say the otherwise un-sayable, and to take on targets that were hitherto deemed unassailable.

But even comedy can be converged.

The September 2019 firing of Shane Gillis from *Saturday Night Live* less than one week after his hiring had been announced by NBC is just one of many examples of the way the social justice cancer has spread from corporations to comedians.

Ironically, less than a year before Patreon's Trust and Safety team was threatening Owen Benjamin with the removal of his account on the basis of its right to police other platforms, its CEO, Jack Conte, was giving public interviews talking about how free and open the platform was for creators, how tolerant the platform was, and how the absence of advertisers meant that creators didn't have to be afraid of being deplatformed for their opinions.

> *Creators watching us, you just don't have to worry about this shit! You just don't have to worry about it! People like you, and most people who are engaging in healthy dialogue and talking about tough issues, this is just not something that concerns most creators. It kills me a little bit that there's this fear. You know, one of the things Sam Harris said in the podcast where he talked about leaving Patreon was that there's this wave of deplatforming; it just kills me that there is that fear there and it doesn't have to be there for most creators....*
>
> *I totally understand how it's legit fear, I just I guess what I was trying to express was that I don't like that fear is associated with Patreon because at the end of the day we just have a very different, we have a much higher tolerance of stuff. We don't have advertisers and that just makes such a big difference, that's why we have been able to do what we do.*
>
> —Jack Conte, *The Rubin Report*, July 31, 2017

However, the decision of the well-known author of *The End of Faith* and *Letter to a Christian Nation* to flee the Patreon platform proved to be perspicacious indeed. In December 2018, Sam Harris, who at the time was the holder of the 11th-largest account on Patreon with 9,000 patrons, voluntarily shut down his account due to his unwillingness to "expose any part of my podcast funding to the whims of Patreon's 'Trust and Safety' committee."

And less than a year after the controversial atheist's departure, Patreon finally followed through on their previous threat. On October 9, 2019, Owen Benjamin's Patreon account was terminated due to what David from Patreon Trust and Safety described as attacking people "on the basis of religion".

*David (Patreon)*

*Oct 9, 4:22 PM PDT*

*Hi Owen,*

*My name is David and I'm on Patreon's Trust & Safety team. I'm writing you to let you know I've removed your creator page for violating the site's Community Guidelines concerning Hate Speech.*

*Patreon endeavors to be a space where thought leaders can engage difficult topics, criticize the powerful and question pervasive ideologies. Patreon doesn't, however, allow creators to propagate negative stereotypes on the basis of status within a protected class, which we communicated to you in emails sent April of last year.*

*In a number of posts since shared on Instagram and in videos you've shared online, you've targeted Jewish people with similar negative stereotypes. Because you've attacked people on the basis of religion, my team and I have removed your creator page.*

*I've paid out your final creator balance in the amount of $5.11.*

*In the future, if you ever want to fund a new project on Patreon that is within the site's guidelines, feel free to contact my team at guidelines@patreon.com. You can also read more about account reinstatement here.*

*If you have any other questions or concerns, please don't hesitate to reach out to me and I'll do my best to address them for you.*

*All the best,*

*Patreon Trust and Safety Monday-Friday*

The list of well-known creators and companies who had either been deplatformed by Patreon Trust and Safety, or who jumped from the platform before they could be pushed, had increased by one. That increasingly long list includes, ironically enough, Dave Rubin, who apparently did not buy Jack Conte's assurances any more than Sam Harris did, as well media figures that range the gamut from Milo Yiannopoulos to Dr. Jordan Peterson.

On October 28, 2019, Owen Benjamin filed for arbitration as per the Patreon Terms of Use.

# Chapter 11

## Legal Encounters:
## The Lessons Learned

While it is not possible to discuss the particulars of our most recent forays into arbitration now, there is no reason I cannot share with you some of the lessons learned by me and one of the members of the Legal Legion of Evil in our legal encounters with various technology and social media companies. These include, but are not limited to, Amazon, Twitter, GoodReads, Google, PayPal, Patreon, GT Interactive, YouTube, and WeFunder.

### 1. Everyone is not out to get you.

Even after deciding legal action was necessary, we were aware that Indiegogo didn't particularly care about us or our comic book series one way or the other. We assumed—incorrectly, as it happened—that the responsible party was an SJW activist working within the corporation, since we had seen that very scenario play out eight separate times inside Amazon. The truth turned out to be rather more complicated and nuanced than the scenario we originally envisioned.

Don't assume the other side is the enemy. They may have found themselves manipulated into that position, but they don't necessarily hate you. They are the opposition; the goal is to defeat them, not destroy them. And remember, their lawyers are only hired guns. They're not the enemy either. A legal dispute is stressful enough without taking everything personally.

## 2. Beware of the back channel communications.

In Silicon Valley circles, everyone knows everyone. This is a slight exaggeration, of course, but if there are six degrees of separation in the real world, there are two degrees of separation, at most, in the international media-technology complex. We were surprised to discover that there were not only direct personal connections between tech companies in the same sector, but also between various media organizations and the tech companies as well as between the independent arbitrators and the tech companies. The technology world is a small one at the higher levels, and word spreads rapidly from company to company, even across continents.

As one Google manager warned conservatives at Google on the company's internal Google+ system, there is a social justice blacklist across the technology sector that extends well beyond Silicon Valley:

- *I will never, ever hire/transfer you onto my team. Ever. I don't care if you are perfect fit or technically excellent, whatever.*
- *I will actively not work with you, even to the point where your team or product is impacted by this decision. I'll communicate why to your manager if it comes up.*
- *You're being blacklisted by people at companies outside of Google. You might not have been aware of this, but people know, people talk. There are always social consequences.*

There isn't anything you can do about all of this intercorporate incest, but you can certainly anticipate turning it to your advantage once you reach the discovery process. It doesn't ever seem to occur to them that anyone will ever have access to their communications, and because they always believe what they are doing is morally justified, they don't see any reason to conceal their actions anyhow.

### 3. Do your research.

Sun Tzu assures us that if you know yourself and you know the enemy, you will not lose, not even if you fight one hundred battles. The more you know about the other side, from their executives to their lawyers, the more that you can get inside their head and see things from their perspective, the easier it is to anticipate their actions. Social media, especially LinkedIn, can be a gold mine in this regard.

### 4. Don't expect the other side's actions to make sense. And above all, do not project!

Corporations are made up of many individuals, and individuals usually have their own agendas and interests that may or may not be in line with what you imagine the corporation's rational interest to be. The average corporate employee sees no connection between his own actions and the company's profits, and even high-ranking executives may be more concerned in burying the evidence of their own mistakes than eliminating serious existential risks to the corporation. Any strategy that relies upon expecting the other side to do as you would in their situation is almost certain to fail.

### 5. The judge is a Magic Eight Ball.

This was possibly the most important lesson that we learned over time. You simply cannot expect a judge, or an arbitrator, to do anything of his own volition. If you want him to do anything, or establish anything, *anything at all*, you have to ask him to specifically rule upon the matter even if you quite reasonably assume that it is already a settled matter of fact. Even things as seemingly iron-clad as the rules that nominally govern the procedure can be subject to interpretation, if not complete reinvention and redefinition, so it is important to always make *direct and specific* requests of the judge rather than assume anything. In the legal context, words and numbers don't mean what they say, they mean what the judge decides they say, so you usually need to ask him to define them.

## 6. Read everything at least three times, on three separate occasions.

In hindsight, it was really remarkable how long it took us to finally work out our most effective strategy. All of the information was right there in front of us from the start, but none of us were in the correct frame of mind at the time to see it until we were months into the process. You will tend to find yourself initially reading the material to confirm your preconceived legal narrative, which is almost certainly going to cause you to miss the key details that will lead you toward a more effective approach. By re-reading both the agreements as well the relevant rules and laws, and by doing so on multiple occasions, you give yourself a much higher probability of recognizing useful elements and thereby honing your strategies and tactics.

## 7. High-priced lawyers are a weakness as well as a weapon.

Bleeding out the other side is a long-favored tactic of Big Law. They know the financial resources of the corporations they represent are one of their biggest advantages and they rely very heavily upon it. This is why having a good lawyer, even a great one, is much less important in these situations than having an affordable one, or better yet, a free one. Especially in consumer arbitration, where a lawyer is not necessarily required, the ability to take this tactic off the table by representing yourself and using a lawyer as a consultant for the necessary filings more than outweighs the disadvantage of initially having no idea what you are doing.

While the pockets of a technology company may seem bottomless, their willingness to pay for billable hours is not. Once they begin to understand that you can afford to play this game as long as they can, they tend to be much more willing to be reasonable and to start looking for a way to bring the conflict to a mutually acceptable end.

This should not be taken as any denigration of the genuine strengths of the high-priced attorneys you may find yourself facing. Their ability to produce reams of relevant case law out of seemingly thin air and to speak in esoteric legalisms that sound like a foreign language is as intimidating as it is astonishing. However, once you begin to see how they tend to be considerably stronger on procedural tactics than they are on overall strategy, and how they are often hamstrung by having to follow directions imposed by the clueless arrogance of their corporate clients, you'll come to realize that you don't have to worry overmuch about their superiority in these regards.

## 8. Communicate the strength of your position, but do not bluff.

Because a legal dispute revolves around presenting two competing narratives to a judge and awaiting the synthesis that he constructs from them, it is understandably hard for the other side to distinguish between the rhetoric of your narrative that supports your case and the dialectic of the cold hard reality that applies no matter what either side happens to believe.

Consider the case of the recent Uber settlement, in which the tech company paid $20 million to its drivers in California and Massachusetts. Uber didn't settle with those 12,501 drivers because it felt it had a weak case, or because it feared that it was going to lose in arbitration, but because, win or lose, it was absolutely committed to spending at least $34,377,750 in filing fees alone, plus another $280 million or so in arbitration fees. Not only was the settlement the only rational way out for Uber, it was very cheap at the price!

Complicating this communications challenge is the fact that even if the other side's lawyers fully comprehend the reality of the situation, it may take them some time to convince their clients that they are trapped between a rock and a hard place. This is why it is so important not to bluff or to exaggerate the strength of your position; the more credibility you have with the opposing lawyers, the easier it is for them to convince their clients of the harsh realities they may be disinclined to accept.

However, some new laws coming into effect in 2020 will tend to mitigate this problem, as they will significantly reduce the time the corporation has to respond before it is held accountable by the legal system.

## 9. Be flexible and expect the unexpected.

No one ever has the full story at the time a legal dispute begins. The narrative you intend to defend may not be quite as accurate as you believe at the start, and some of the supposed facts upon which you constructed it may turn out to be misunderstandings or complete inventions. People have always exaggerated, inflated their own importance, and lied, but social media increases the temptation to do so for many of its users, and so it is vital to be careful of putting too much stock in anything anyone, even a completely impartial party, happens to say in public.

Sometimes what you discover will be useful to your narrative, sometimes it will render an entire theory moot. Either way, you need to be sure that you are not relying anything that may turn out to have flimsy foundations.

## 10. Recon by filing.

Arbitration is unexplored territory for most people, even for highly experienced lawyers. Only a few hundred consumer arbitrations are filed in any given year and most of them are related to credit card debt, so the average corporate lawyer has never even taken part in one. The arbitration rules are vague to the point of being occasionally misleading, the arbitrators can be capricious, and there is no such thing as precedent from one arbitration to the next. No amount of research and reading will suffice to prepare you for what you're going to experience, so the best way to learn how your particular arbitrator prefers to operate is to file one or two early filings upon which he has to rule. Doing this will not only tell you a lot about the arbitrator, but also provide you with a considerable amount of information about the lawyers acting on behalf of the other side.

## 11. Even the biggest whale fears the piranha.

If you read the Terms of Use, or Terms and Conditions, of any technology or social media company, one thing you will notice is that they are absolutely terrified of class actions. This is because the risk of losing a class action lawsuit or arbitration is actual harm to their bottom line, whereas they can easily weather the expense of losing an individual legal dispute. This risk is compounded by the low cost of individual entry to a class action; unlike an individual lawsuit, where one individual is forced to bankroll all the expenses of the filing fees, the lawyers, and the potential costs associated with losing, a participant in a class action seldom risks anything substantial.

This is why forced arbitration is now a standard clause in most terms of use.

However, although most of them do not realize it yet, the tech and social media corporations are now trapped between the Scylla of class action lawsuits and the Charybdis of mass individual arbitrations. While the anticipated addition of forced consolidation clauses may eventually permit corporations to avoid the Uber dilemma in arbitration, all that will accomplish is to create a new form of inexpensive class action that will tend to significantly increase the costs of losing a legal dispute, with one key difference. And that difference is that many state consumer arbitration laws, unlike the court system, do not permit a corporation to charge its legal costs and lawyers fees to the consumers, even when it wins the arbitration.

## 12. Jaw, jaw is better than war, war.

Harold Macmillan's famous dictum, usually attributed incorrectly to Winston Churchill, is extremely applicable here. 80 percent of all arbitrations end up as settlements in the end, so a considerable amount of time, money, and stress can potentially be avoided if both sides simply communicate honestly with the other.

## A Lawyer's Reflections on Big Tech

I asked a friend and colleague who has been intimately involved in our legal disputes to share a few of his thoughts on the subject. He is a very experienced lawyer with credentials that you probably wouldn't believe even if I shared them with you, which I won't. He is also the senior managing partner of the Legal Legion of Evil.

---

Many conservatives think of the major tech companies as proactively and zealously pushing a progressive and Leftist agenda. And Big Tech certainly is guilty of doing so. Big Tech can afford to push an agenda that is unpopular with the majority of their users; insulated by their massive market caps and given cover by their media cheerleaders. They are, almost uniformly, so converged that they now subordinate profit-making to the pushing of the social justice agenda.

But most companies are not thought leaders; they are actually followers. For every Eye of Soros-authorized tech giant like Facebook or Google, there are countless NPC zombies, who mindlessly follow the current media narrative. Whatever the predominant political zeitgeist happens to be at the moment, they ape it. They blindly follow the path of least resistance, all the while basking in the praise and perceived status that comes from their wokeness and virtue-signaling.

This is not to say they *disagree* with the progressive agenda. They almost certainly agree with the thought leaders who set and drive the agenda, but not because they have thought their way through the merits of that agenda. They aren't that reflective, they aren't that intellectually curious, and most of all, they are not truth-seekers. Their viewpoint is often the result of indoctrination rather than conviction. They are easily manipulated and influenced themselves, and they simply want to virtue-signal, be applauded for their bravery and go about their business without getting into any trouble.

It was proverbially said of fund managers "No one ever got fired for buying IBM." For the average tech company manager today, "No one ever got fired for deplatforming a 'Nazi' " could be their mantra. (Well, that's no longer true, but I digress…)

In practice, at many tech companies, the people who most strongly support or are amenable to social justice are given significant free reign even where the corporation is not primarily driven by social justice. This is simply the way things are done. This approach is applauded by the media, consumer groups, shareholders and many other "stakeholders", so in recent years there has been little risk or downside to pursuing this strategy. It is the easy thing to do, the path of least resistance, and an approach that will usually get them praised for their wokeness, bravery and virtue.

Unless and until, that is, people push back against it. The current default mode of Woke Social Justice in the boardroom only functions if that mode is easy and costless for a company. The more people push back and make it difficult and costly for them to pursue an agenda of social justice, the more we weaken them, the more we learn their vulnerabilities, and the more we make it more likely that they will have to change their ways or be replaced by competitors.

What are some of the implications and lessons from our experiences with various deplatformings and battles against corporate cancer?

## 1. Build your own platforms.

Even if social justice is not a primary goal of the top management of an organization, O'Sullivan's Law and the law of social justice convergence are in effect: The influence of SJWs within trust and safety and other departments, and the predictable pusillanimity of most others within the organization means that, for all intents and purposes, most companies are actively *opposed* to any dissident or non-mainstream perspective that questions or challenges the progressive worldview. So resistance and rejection from platforms that are not your own or do not explicitly support Free Speech or Dissident Right ideas, will continue to be the norm. Thus, building our own platforms and establishing alliances with, and supporting, true allies remain pillars of pursuing and promoting your own projects.

## 2. SJWs do not expect pushback.

The Left's deplatforming, depersoning, and discrediting attacks on the Right have become so formulaic and standardized that they—quite understandably—do not expect serious pushback or resistance in response to their actions. The defining characteristic of the most famous victims of deplatforming is publicly crying to the media and complaining about the unfairness of it all. But most deplatformed individuals and institutions simply accept their fate and project the burden onto the Department of Justice or some other unnamed authority to step in and white-knight for them. When SJWs actually receive pushback, they are caught *extremely* off-guard. They simply aren't ready for the conflict because they so seldom experience any that puts them on the defensive. If you strike back, you can put yourself on the offensive and keep them off-balance. Be Trump, not Jeb. Please clap.

## 3. Top management is likely in the dark about the situation.

The autonomy enjoyed by SJWs within an organization combined with the usual lack of pushback by their victims means that communications between top management and the people enforcing the policies on the ground may be infrequent and not entirely forthcoming. Management assumes everything is on autopilot, because it usually is. And when it isn't, the last thing an SJW will want is for her superior to know that things are not going accordingly to plan. So the lines of communication within an organization are often inefficient, slow and not forthcoming. When the reality of the situation becomes known, an unconverged top management may end up acting far more rationally in a way that serves the business, not an agenda. However, the SJW's desire to keep his actions hidden may well delay necessary communications that could resolve a situation. In fact, greater conflict and escalation of a conflict could mean that management is out of the loop and does not know what is occurring.

## 4. A level battlefield does not favor them.

In the 2016 election, the media, the pollsters, academia, the political establishment, and other elites placed themselves in a self-reinforcing delusion bubble that ignored the actual sentiment of the electorate. Hence their total shock at the result. Likewise, the tech companies, who have the media, academia, political interests and other influential institutions reliably on their side, can amplify their point of view and lead everyone to overestimate their strength and resilience. But when the battle takes place outside of their preferred venues, they lose these advantages and many of their go-to weapons become utterly useless. Journalists may not care about contracts and law, only about Who and Whom, but the same cannot always be said of a court, a tribunal, a mediator, or an arbitrator, particularly one who is not beholden to Silicon Valley. When the tech companies are forced to fight outside of their comfort zones, away from the protective arms of their powerful allies, and find themselves engaged on more objective and level battlefields, they quickly discover that many of their standard tactics will not work. And more often than not, they don't have a Plan B.

## 5. Make the rubble bounce.

Even if you are unable to win an encounter, always make sure the company comes to regret its decision to cause a problem for you. The more cost there is to a converged company for deplatforming someone, or for denying a customer service, the more likely its executives are to see what a bad business practice it is. And seeing how much money corporate cancer is costing them may, in some circumstances, lead the wise executive to steer his organization away from social justice and toward serving its primary business purpose in the future. And if it doesn't, and the executives decide to double down, corporate cancer will harm their bottom line in the long run and make them far more vulnerable to competition with unconverged rivals.

# Chapter 12

## What the Future Holds

Things can't help but look increasingly dire to the average businessman or consumer who surveys the U.S. and global society today. Most of the elements that made up the stable, prosperous geopolitical environment and international economy during the post-World War II period have now either vanished or are rapidly crumbling. Science, technology, and law have all been converged in varying degrees, mutually-agreed-upon contracts have been replaced by unilaterally-imposed end user license agreements, quality has been abandoned in favor of the lowest cost solutions, the U.S. is locked in a long-overdue trade war with China and others who have exploited the West's foolish free trade policies, the European Union is breaking apart, democracy is being traduced by globalists desperate to maintain the failing neo-liberal world order, freedom of speech and expression is being repressed by techno-fascists, and nationalists are rising to power everywhere from Austria to India.

At the present, all that maintains the current system is $184 trillion in global debt, 250 million international migrants, and the United States military. And all three of these remaining elements of the post-WWII order are increasingly tending to add to the instability of the system instead of mitigating it.

What this means is that the business environment is going to continue to change, and, most likely, undergo a serious transformation even more significant than we previously witnessed with the rise of the Information Society and the Internet economy.

Consider the state of Silicon Valley, perhaps the primary ingredient in that massive evolution that sparked revolutions in communication, travel, trade, migration, and entertainment around the world.

Most people believe that Silicon Valley has never been more powerful or influential. The reality is that thanks to the near-complete convergence of the technology giants, the incompetence of their untested legal departments, and the foolish behavior of the ironically-named Trust and Safety departments at those companies, Silicon Valley has never been more vulnerable to large-scale disruption.

In fact, I would go so far as to observe that Silicon Valley as we know it is unlikely to survive more than five years if it does not change its ways, and change them very fast. Corporate cancer is killing the technology goose that laid the golden eggs that have changed the lives of billions of people around the world.

More than a few people in the industry are already aware the current situation is fundamentally unstable, even though none of them yet recognize the most dire existential threat of the various difficulties they presently are facing. Among these are the way the U.S. government is beginning to cast a skeptical eye on the monopolistic practices of the larger companies like Google and Facebook as well as the publisher/platform dance being performed by companies seeking to simultaneously police their users while trying to avoid being held responsible for their site content, the way Apple and other hardware manufacturers are getting caught up in the U.S.-China trade war, the Great Firewall of China and other restrictions on cross-border Internet traffic, and the way a number of European countries are starting to pass laws to specifically address the various abuses committed by the Big Tech corporations.

And there are a plethora of abuses being committed, from transparent schemes to avoid paying taxes to open ideological and religious discrimination. For example, in an interview with a Polish magazine, a PayPal executive in Poland admitted that he is fully aware that the politically motivated deplatformings by his organization are illegal, and that he expects PayPal will eventually have to restore the accounts of those who have been deplatformed, but he still expects PayPal to continue deplatforming those of whom the organization disapproves in order to maximize the damage it causes them.

It is not about the money, the executive says, thereby confirming once more the central thesis of this book. And not long after the interview, PayPal placed payment restrictions on a Catholic publishing house in Poland:

> *On behalf of the editorial staff of Magna Polonia, P. Przemysław Holocher explains that the publishing house has been harassed for a long time by global concerns such as Facebook and Google.*
>
> *"Facebook continues to limit our posts and block our accounts. I am also convinced that we will soon disappear from this portal. YouTube imposes advertising restrictions on each of our videos, which means we can't earn anything. Google ads have been limited, we have been banned from using the most effective form of advertising, i.e. tracking users by interests. Reason? We have religious books in the store," writes Mr Holocher.*
>
> *Now it's time to hit the publisher's finances. The PayPal payment system has announced that the foundation's account has permanent restrictions.*

—"PayPal has hit Magna Polonia", October 6, 2019

It would be hard to cite a more typical example of corporate cancer in action.

The new European laws and regulations are hitting the tech giants hard. In just the last two years, the European Union has forced Google to pay €8.2 billion in fines for a series of antitrust violations that may presage similar fines in the United States and elsewhere. In April 2019, France passed the first law imposing a three-percent tax on corporations that use consumer data to sell online advertising, have annual global sales of over €750 million, and revenue exceeding €25 million euros in France. This tax is expected to affect 30 multinationals, but is known as the GAFA Act due to its specific targeting of Google, Apple, Facebook, and Amazon.

Spain and the United Kingdom quickly followed suit by passing similar Internet taxes on the technology giants. Other countries will almost certainly imitate the three European nations, either to raise their tax revenues or protect their smaller domestic alternatives. The age of Silicon Valley's free ride is officially over.

But these various threats pale in comparison to the multiple vulnerabilities that have been created by the combination of legal and Trust and Safety overstretch on the part of the converged consumer platforms and payment processors, which has left all of Silicon Valley wide open to massive financial devastation and disruption on a cataclysmic scale. It is an understatement to say that the risk is existential in nature.

The first, and lesser, risk, is primarily strategic. China, and now Russia, have successfully fenced off their national Internet economies and are actively fostering strong domestic competitors to the U.S.-based technology giants. In China, Rénrénwang, Alibaba, Baidu, TenCent, Taobao, and Sina Weibo have replaced Facebook, Amazon, Google, YouTube, eBay, and Twitter. While the Russian alternatives are not as comprehensive or as large as their Chinese counterparts, social media sites like Vkontakte, Yandex, OK, and Moi Mir were already holding their own before Russia began to install RuNet, the Russian version of the Great Chinese Firewall.

What these national firewalls do is provide the Russian and Chinese technology companies a safe and stable foundation from which they can launch competitive incursions into the established markets of Europe and the United States, as well as into the less mature markets of Brazil, India, and other countries. Compounding the Sino-Russian competitive advantage is the way in which the converged U.S. technology giants are making their products less and less attractive to their users while simultaneously frightening off a significant portion of their existing customer base with their incessant deplatformings and demonetizations. To put it in economic turns, on the one hand they are reducing the demand for their products, while on the other, they are restricting the supply. It does not require a sophisticated mastery of the Supply-Demand Curve to grasp the way in which this behavior is not at all conducive to increasing market share, revenues, or profits in the future.

Meanwhile, their Chinese and Russian competitors, some of whom already possess larger user bases than they do, are increasingly well-positioned to enter their home markets.

## Case Study: PayPal

*Probably the most important value to us is diversity and inclusion.*

—PayPal CEO Dan Schulman

Consider, for example, the current situation in the payment processing market. PayPal is the dominant Silicon Valley corporation, with 286 million active registered accounts and $15.5 billion in annual revenue. On November 5, 2019, PayPal publicly announced that it was shutting down the account of Stefan Molyneux, a popular independent YouTuber with 929k subscribers and 439k Twitter followers, saying "After conducting an extensive review, PayPal has made the decision to discontinue our business relationship with Stefan Molyneux."

PayPal can obviously survive without Stefan Molyneux's business. It can survive without any of the "10 to 20" accounts its Trust and

Safety employees ban every week, according to one of its executives. But think about the impression that its action has made on Molyneux's hundreds of thousands of loyal followers, most of whom almost certainly have active PayPal accounts. Even if they only represent three-tenths of one percent of PayPal's customers, that is an awful lot of clients to needlessly antagonize with just one decision, particularly in light of the chilling effect it will have on other outspoken individuals with similarly large followings.

Now contemplate the fact that a foreign payment processor owned by a company that is more than four times larger than PayPal already has more than 7,000 locations set up across the United States, including 3,000 Walgreen's stores. While Alipay is presently focused on serving the payment needs of Chinese tourists and students studying abroad, its ambitions to penetrate Western markets will inevitably lead it to pursue Western customers before long; it has already begun offering its services to Western tourists in China. In the meantime, PayPal is driving millions of its existing customers away and into the arms of the first payment processor who will welcome them with promises of safe harbor.

*We heard you. You want to use Alipay and guess what? Now you can! Visitors to China are now able to #PayWithAlipay. Simply download Alipay via app stores to start enjoying wallet-free travel!*

*—A Guide to Alipay for International Travelers in China*

Can you guess who will be happy to welcome those unwanted Western customers? And what do you think the result of the ensuing global competition is going to be when Alipay, or TenCent's WeChat, realizes that it can readily sweep up half of the U.S. payment market without PayPal being able to compete effectively in the Chinese market? It will make what FoxNews did to CNN in the Nielsen ratings look merciful in comparison.

And, as we've seen, thanks to PayPal's aggressive deplatforming policy, precisely the same dynamic will apply in European markets from Poland to the United Kingdom.

Ironically, the one hope here for Big Tech giants like PayPal is if the U.S. government is willing to intervene in order to protect them from dominant foreign competitors. But why should President Trump, or any Republican senator or congressman, lift a finger to assist the very corporations that are aggressively deplatforming their supporters, their voters, and in some cases, even threatening to ban the politicians themselves?

But perhaps the strangest thing about PayPal's decision to deplatform its Western account holders is that it is obviously aware of the danger posed to it by the competition from China. While it recently received approval from China's central bank to take a controlling interest in a small Chinese payments provider called GoPay, as the Chief Economist at ING Asia observes, "China tends to only open up markets when it thinks domestic firms already have it pretty much stitched up and aren't too worried about the competition."

Given that Alibaba and TenCent control 90 percent of the market between them, there is no reason to believe that PayPal will be any more successful in China than eBay, Amazon, or Google were.

## Silicon Valley's ticking time-bomb

As daunting as the looming competition for market dominance in the various tech sectors looks to be, there is actually a much more serious, and much more imminent, threat to the big dogs of Silicon Valley. This second threat is existential, it is now, to a certain extent, unavoidable, and it is entirely self-inflicted.

The problem was created by a combination of arrogance and innocence on the part of the founders of the various technology start-ups; it is in part a cultural legacy of the Silicon Valley belief in its special status combined with the difficulty of applying laws written for a trade in material goods and services to the Internet. The decision of the various government agencies and state revenue departments to more or less leave the Internet economy alone seems to have instilled in most technology executives the core belief that the law simply did not apply to them.

It is a common belief on the part of many users of Internet platforms that the terms of use that are imposed upon the user of a site, a product, or a service are the whole of the relevant law. But this is only true when nothing of value is being exchanged, such as in the case of Twitter. After all, one can hardly claim to have been materially harmed by one's inability to continue to receive services of literally zero value.

Many of the tech giants became massive through offering free services to the public and selling the data thus acquired to other corporations and the government. Once they were established and publicly traded, they came under heavy pressure to produce more revenue by monetizing their popular consumer services, which many of them have done to varying degrees. However, they never modified their mindset or their legal contracts—which is what their "terms of use" and "terms of service" are—to take into account the fact that many of their activities were now subject to centuries of well-established contract law.

Even worse, they sought to avoid any responsibility for the separate relationship between the parties that they were bringing together in their online marketplaces. For example, Airbnb made their lack of involvement in the separate contract between its creators and their contributors explicit in their Terms of Use effective November 1, 2019:

*When Members make or accept a booking, they are entering into a contract directly with each other. Airbnb is not and does not become a party to or other participant in any contractual relationship between Members, nor is Airbnb a real estate broker or insurer. Airbnb is not acting as an agent in any capacity for any Member, except as specified in the Payments Terms.*

In other words, what they increasingly did is create situations where they were making their money by bringing two parties together and taking a small part of the transaction of the separate legal agreement between those two parties. That's how Uber works, that's how PayPal works, that's how Kickstarter works, that's how YouTube works, that's how Airbnb works, and so forth. You get the point.

This is a valuable service they are providing, and most of these companies well merit the revenue they derive from bringing buyers and sellers, passengers and drivers, creators and contributors, hosts and guests, together in an easy and efficient manner. The problem is that as a non-participant in the separate legal agreement between those two parties, they do not possess any right to interfere in that separate agreement regardless of what their Terms of Use happen to say. And the tech companies did not—in fact, still do not—realize this.

There is a word for when a third party interferes in a separate contract between two parties to which it is not a party. And that word is "tortious interference".

What this means is that every time a tech company like Kickstarter or PayPal or Airbnb interferes with an existing arrangement between two parties that costs one or both of the parties any money, it becomes at least potentially legally liable for the harm it has caused to them.

Most of the time, this potential liability is irrelevant. The sums involved are usually far too small to justify the time and expense of a lawsuit, and very few individuals are crazy enough to want to take on a huge tech company that has full-time lawyers and what appear to be near-infinite resources. Even so, because they were aware of the large numbers of consumers using their services, the lawyers for the tech companies were very careful to prevent the possibility of anyone lodging a class action lawsuit against them. If you ever bother to read the Terms of Use of a tech site, you will almost invariably come across a clause requiring you to waive your right to pursue class action if you wish to use the site. PayPal's anti-class action clause from their Terms of Use effective September 3, 2019 is very typical in this regard.

*You and PayPal agree that each of us may bring claims against the other only on an individual basis and not as a plaintiff or class member in any purported class or representative action or proceeding. Unless both you and PayPal agree otherwise, the arbitrator(s) may not consolidate or join more than one person's or party's claims and may not otherwise preside over any form of a consolidated, representative or class proceeding.*

Notice the reference to "the arbitrator(s)". This, too, is very typical, as with a few exceptions such as Google, Kickstarter, and Twitter, most tech companies unilaterally impose arbitration on their users, thereby ensuring that they will not find themselves caught up in an endless series of long and expensive lawsuits. Arbitration tends to be much less expensive than the courts, and usually serves as a sort of home-court advantage for the corporations that utilize it, as the authors of NBER Working Paper No. 25150, entitled *Arbitration with Uninformed Consumers* and issued in October 2018, declared after examining the results of nearly 10,000 consumer arbitration cases:

*This paper argues that firms have an informational advantage over consumers in selecting arbitrators in consumer arbitration. We document how the selection process impacts arbitration outcomes by studying roughly 9,000 consumer arbitration cases in the securities industry. Securities disputes present a good laboratory: arbitration is mandatory for all disputes, eliminating selection concerns; the parties choose arbitrators from a randomly generated list, and arbitrators are compensated only if chosen; and the selection mechanism is similar to other major arbitration forums. We document three facts. First, some arbitrators are systematically more industry friendly than others. Second, firms appear to exploit this information: despite a randomly generated list of potential arbitrators, industry-friendly arbitrators are forty percent more likely to be selected. Third, more experienced firms and less sophisticated consumers select more industry friendly arbitrators.*

However, what appears to be a series of stacked advantages for the tech companies turns out, upon deeper study, to be a fatal flaw. In fact, when one puts all the pieces of the puzzle together—and I will refrain from doing so here for various reasons that should be obvious— it becomes abundantly clear that the majority of the tech giants and social media companies in Silicon Valley can be bankrupted at will within 45 days by a number of individuals acting in concert.

This is not a hypothesis. This is not a theory. This is a plain and proven statement about a legal approach that has already been repeatedly utilized to devastating effect to the tune of up to eight digits.

The question is a simple and straightforward one. Will Silicon Valley collectively choose to mend its wicked ways, do its job, and stop attempting to play thought police for the entire world? Or will it implode by imposing the form of its destructor?

## Debt, diversity, and the Devil Mouse

Investors often say that which cannot continue will not. But as one influential economist who was also a highly successful investor noted, "the market can stay irrational longer than you can stay solvent." So, we can't expect to know exactly when a converged company is going to succumb to the corporate cancer that has infested it. There is an awful lot of ruin in companies as big and resource-rich as Apple, Disney, Google, Intel, or Microsoft; a single disaster, or even a single series of disasters is probably not going to be sufficient to do them in.

But if the precise end of a converged company cannot be foreseen, the beginning of the endgame often can be. This is because a corporate failure cascade, or a process in a system of interconnected parts in which the failure of one or more parts triggers the failure of other parts, is often observable by even casual observers.

For example, Disney looks indomitable when seen from a distance. It has a market capitalization of nearly $250 billion and in 2018 reported an annual profit of $12.6 billion on $59.4 billion in revenue. It owns a veritable gold mine of intellectual property, from Mickey Mouse to *Star Wars*, and is arguably the most formidable entertainment empire in the history of the world to date.

But look a little closer and a less imposing picture begins to take form. In just the last year, Disney's debt has increased by $38 billion, to a total of $53 billion now owed. And while that figure is low by considered low by industry standards, it has amassed that gargantuan debt to pay for projects that are already failing at an rate that is extremely uncharacteristic of historical Disney projects.

Consider, too, that Netflix now owes $12.4 billion in debt with $15.8 billion in annual revenue, so despite Disney's low debt/equity ratio of 0.38, it has a debt/revenue rate of 89.2 percent, which is actually higher than the notoriously unstable Netflix's 78.4 percent.

*Star Wars* isn't the only one of Disney's once-dominant properties and franchises that are failing. The two Galaxy's Edge theme parks were failures at launch, attendance is declining at both its flagship parks, and ESPN has been losing two million subscribers a year for the last seven years.

Although it has ridden the Marvel Cinematic Universe—which it did not create—to record-breaking box office heights, its attempt to mine its rich cartoon franchise for live action films has not panned out very well when corrected for inflation—the 1994 Lion King made $178 million more than its 2019 remake—and its attempts to create new franchises that can be similarly exploited have repeatedly failed.

On the other hand, Disney is still generating mammoth products, its seemingly endless series of remakes are profitable, and the launch of its new Disney+ streaming channel could lead to a whole new period of growth for the entertainment giant. Then again, the decision to retroactively censor old films from *Song of the South* to *Dumbo* and

*The Lady and the Tramp* tends to suggest that convergence will cause Disney+ to disappoint too.

In the end, it is probable CEO Bob Iger's declaration that the corporation's push for more diversity in its entertainment products will be followed by an increase of diversity in its executive suite before he retires that will prove the most reliable guide for the future of Disney as well as a test of the central thesis of this book.

There are only three possibilities, after all. Either social justice convergence is beneficial for business, it is harmful for business, or it is irrelevant. And at this point, it should be eminently clear that is about as good for the average corporation as cancer.

Are we seeing the beginning of a series of convergence-related failure cascades across corporate America? Disney may prove to be a useful harbinger in this regard.

## Excising the cancer

Addressing the specifics on how to excise convergence from a corporation could be a book, or more usefully, a consulting service in its own right. But in the current absence of the latter, the most important aspect of transforming yourself into a cost-cutting, profit-protecting corporate surgeon is steel in your spine. You must attack the problem with all the vigor and self-confidence of a fireman putting out a fire in a burning house.

The corporation's cancer cells will seek to protect themselves and maintain their influence over the corporation. First they will try to excise you, and if that doesn't work, they will try to hide, professing innocence, good intentions, and promises to do better.

Do not believe them!

Your chief ally in slashing away at the cancer in your organization will be the accounting department. Because convergence is reliably expensive and non-productive, simply forcing each department to quantify its contributions to the bottom line will quickly tell you where the converged employees are concentrated. However, the worst departments, Human Resources, Marketing, and Legal, are somewhat insulated due to the fact that their activities are not expected to con-tributed directly to the revenues of the corporation.

This is where performance metrics that apply to their non-revenue producing activities will prove to be useful. Remember the example of the Restoration Hardware CEO who eliminated his online mar-keting budget—and presumably reduced the size of his marketing department—when he discovered that all of their efforts were of no effect whatsoever? There are always some relevant metrics that you can find, and if you can't find any that suit your purposes, invent them!

Converged employees tend to spend a considerable amount of their workday on political activism. For example, many women and diversi-ties in tech devote most of their time talking about the need for more women and diversities in tech, their own obvious non-productivity notwithstanding. For example, it is not at all unheard of for in-house counsel to hand off all responsibility for the corporation's legal disputes to outside lawyers, then jet off to conferences to give speeches on why more women in the company's market sector are necessary.

A simple review of the average HR or marketing employee's time-stamped social media during office hours will be sufficient to jettison a statistically-significant portion of the company's converged personnel. Sure, they might have legitimate job-related reasons to be on LinkedIn, or Facebook, or Twitter, or posting on the company intranet, but are the anti-Trump memes and rainbow advocacy virtue-signals really part of their job description?

As it is written, seek and ye shall find.

Another very useful resource will be the employee handbook and code of conduct. Because corporate activists blithely assume—not entirely without reason—that the rules will not be applied to them in any circumstances, they frequently violate them openly and without hesitation. Just to give one of many possible examples of this corporate hypocrisy, Point 4 of Google's code of conduct addresses threats of violence in the workplace.

### 4. Safe Workplace

*We are committed to a violence-free work environment, and we will not tolerate any level of violence or the threat of violence in the workplace.*

This straightforward statement by Google did not stop its converged employees from publicly threatening to "silence" and even "punch" their fellow employees who happened to hold "different political views" in the aftermath of the James Damore controversy. One manager even said he wanted "to burn the building to the ground." But the reason they got away with such egregious violations of their corporate code of conduct was because no one held them accountable to it.

If you are in a sufficiently senior position to hold converged employees to account, one of the most productive things you can do for your organization is to compare their behavior to the organization's code of conduct in a methodical and ruthless manner. If you are not in a senior position, filing regular complaints against converged individuals may not be enough to eject them from the organization, but it is an excellent means of inoculating yourself against future attacks on you.

Nothing sends a stronger signal that you are not going to be a pushover than a strong and well-evidenced documentary assault on a corporate cancer cell. Converged individuals tend to be cowards who shrink from direct conflict, so once they know that you are willing and able to go after their job, they will be inclined to leave you alone to do yours.

Just watch your back. Once alerted to the fact that you are a hard target, they will always be looking for the opportunity to take a safe shot at you. Don't give them the opportunity.

## You are the cavalry

One of the reasons the corporations of America have been converged so completely in the last two decades is that most of those who understood the intrinsic dangers to the bottom line posed by tolerance, equality, progress, inclusivity, and diversity refused to do anything to stop the metastasizing of these corporate cancers. Their organizations have suffered greatly as a result, and all for the want of courage to stand up for the material interests of the corporation's stakeholders.

Stop waiting for someone to ride to your rescue. You are not helpless, and no one else has as much to gain, or to lose, as you do. The situation is not going to improve on its own, so you have two choices. Either hunker down, hope for the best, and hope that there is enough ruin in your organization to last until you reach retirement age, or embrace the conflict, excise the cancer, and profit accordingly.

Across the West, the cancer of social justice convergence is killing corporations. Because you have read this book, you are among the few, the proud, and the aware, who are capable of stopping it in your organization.

There is a mantra I regularly recite to the Evil Legion of Evil. Perhaps you will find a modicum of the inspiration in it that they do.

*Conflict is the air we breathe. Conflict is the water in which we swim.*

Don't fear the conflict, embrace it! Excise the cancer from your corporation. Be the cavalry and ride to the rescue of your colleagues and coworkers. And then reap the professional benefits that will accrue to you as a result.

# Appendix

## In Which I Express A Heartfelt Apology To *Rolling Stone* Journalist Amanda Robb

## by Pax Dickinson

A fortnight ago I was contacted by a Ms. Amanda Robb, who identified herself as a journalist. Having had a personal history of difficulty with unsavory wretches of that sort, and being a well-known proponent of a harsh criminal punishment for their un-American collectivist scribblings, I of course immediately recommended that Ms. Robb engage in a vigorous act of self-procreation.

Ms. Robb, however, would not be deterred. She (I did not ask her pronoun, regrettably, so I must assume) was earnestly seeking my comment regarding traditionalist superhero comic books and the manners and methods of aggregating funds for the production of such. The aggressively persistent Ms. Robb told me she is a journalist for the widely known (none would say 'popular', but it is widely known) *Rolling Stone* magazine; which magazine, I learned, is not actually solely published for manipulative character assassinations of washed-up entertainers and the dissemination of libelous false rape accusations against innocent frat boys, but purports to do Actual Journalism. I questioned this ambition, of course, but Ms. Robb assured me that the former incautious *Rolling Stone* editors responsible for the recent libelous rape fiction had been quite thoroughly sacked after the massive financial settlement and had been replaced by a new crop of editors who were assuredly much cleverer about not being found responsible for making things up in any legally actionable way.

Upon perusing Ms. Robb's prior work at *Marie Claire*, *The Guardian* and with *The Investigative Fund of The Nation Magazine*, which focused on baby-killing tips, a convenient debunking of investigations of elite pedophile rings, and Ms. Robb's personal experiences with extensive plastic surgery, I could only conclude Ms. Robb must be undoubtedly amongst the finest of politically axe-grinding journalists working in stale Boomer left-wing pop music magazines today.

I explained to Ms. Robb that I have retired to the quiet life of a simple gentleman farmer, knew and cared little about comic books, and did not seek further attention from the media-propaganda complex. I further explained that I considered her employers and her "profession" (such that it is) to be distasteful at best and criminal at worst, and that I expected she might not have the best of intentions toward me given my knowledge about how modern journalism is done and my past experiences being a subject of the yellow press. I directly and forthrightly informed Ms. Robb that I considered her to be my enemy and refused to help her. Ms. Robb, however, was not to be discouraged by any such declaration.

Ms. Robb insisted on an interview despite my pugnacious resistance and emphatically asserted that it would be helpful for her story. Worn down by her insipid pleadings, I reluctantly agreed, and set up a meeting with her in New York City for the next afternoon. I wasn't in New York City, and in fact I was at my home over one hundred miles away from New York City. I had absolutely no ability or plans to be in New York City by that next day, but Ms. Robb was so insistent that I decided to just make the appointment with her and hope for the best.

At the appointed time, for security reasons, I texted Ms. Robb to change the location to a different one at which I hoped to somehow be, despite never having left my home, which is, as I said, over one hundred miles away. She "never got" my message until she was home, so it all worked out. Except for the small detail of actually doing an interview. I was quite comfortable with this outcome but regrettably Ms. Robb was less than satisfied.

I explained to Ms. Robb that I lived over one hundred miles away from New York City and I wasn't planning any trips to New York City in the foreseeable future, so any interview was simply impossible. Ms. Robb immediately suggested driving the three hours to rural Pennsylvania to talk to me. I demurred, but she explained that comic books and the manners and methods of procuring funds for the production of such was of such importance, she would gladly drive over one hundred miles to talk to me despite my repeated professions of ignorance and declarations of refusal to help.

I agreed but explained that I required significant security measures for meetings with the disreputable journalist class she represented, and she would have to follow my security directives to the letter in order to get her interview.

First, I ordered her to purchase a bright red Make America Great Again hat at Trump Tower before her trip. I explained that the fashionable hat would cost $35 due to its quality American-made construction, but assured her that her paymasters at *Rolling Stone* magazine would certainly reimburse her. I explained that I needed her to have the hat for identification purposes later. I also sent her an address to a closed restaurant 3 hours drive from New York and told her to go to that location and await further instructions.

On the appointed date, she eventually arrived, later than the expected time as is the wont of her gender and profession, but arrived nonetheless. I directed her to the next rendezvous point, a small restaurant with outdoor seating 30 minutes drive further west. I told her that upon arrival at this location, she should sit outside and send me a 'selfie' with the red MAGA hat on, in order to confirm her arrival and help me identify her.

At this point, the entire endeavor had been going precisely according to plan, so I'm not sure what explains Ms. Robb's clear expression of annoyance in the selfie I received. Perhaps she had a premonition of the unfortunate disappointment to come, via some oracular power, as some of the distaff sex have been known to possess. However, given the remainder of this tale, Ms. Robb's psychic ability seems scant.

I directed Ms. Robb up the hill and to a pleasant location near the lake in the nearby State Park where I imagine that I might have waited, had I actually left my house, which I hadn't. She expressed reluctance, and then seemingly became confused, sending me a picture of a park sign at the shale pit instead of the lake.

As if a knowledgeable and well-placed journalistic source like myself would imagine hanging out in a dusty shale pit. In retrospect, I suppose a state park with dozens of ambiguous signs marking half a dozen non-interconnecting entrances and extremely spotty cell phone service was not the best choice of rendezvous location. By the time Ms. Robb had arrived at the exact location where I had imagined I might be, I unfortunately was no longer imagining myself there anymore. I certainly tried my best to find Ms. Robb, despite never having left my house, which was, as I said, over a dozen miles away from the park.

Having imagined myself in a place with such spotty cell phone service, I was unable to reply to Ms. Robb's repeated messages looking for me until quite a while later. When I was able to imagine myself in better conditions, I found that she had meandered all over the park in a futile attempt to find the place I had imagined I might be. After a distinct lack of success she then booked a nearby hotel room and informed me that she was prepared to await a more auspicious outcome on the morrow. Not wanting to disappoint, I proposed a very early 6:30 a.m. meeting at Cracker Barrel for the next morning, which Ms. Robb graciously accepted.

Unfortunately, that breakfast was to remain one cracker short of a barrel. In an unforeseen turn of events, I was hypothetically summoned at sunrise to aid a neighbor in rounding up a dozen escaped hogs.

Engaged as I was in these pretend porcine shenanigans, I quite reasonably missed the time for my breakfast meeting with Ms. Robb. I communicated my regrets to her shortly thereafter. She asked if we could instead meet that afternoon but I suggested meeting that evening after I had sufficiently recovered from my swine herding efforts.

That night I changed the time of our dinner from 7:30 p.m. to 9:00 p.m., on a whim, just to keep Ms. Robb entertained. At this time she informed me that her editors were getting irritated. The thought of the finest political editors in the Boomer Left pop music magazine business being personally irritated with my humble antics left me filled with amused pity. Later, I messaged Ms. Robb to tell her I had been delayed by a henway. She not unreasonably asked, "What's a henway?" to which I of course replied, "About three pounds." She didn't understand this, and then began to rudely question my subsequent promise to arrive in a "BOFA" (Brisk Or Fast Arrival—a well-known acronym).

I finally decided that I had had enough of the rudeness of the press for that day, and let her know that the only BOFA she should be expecting was BOFA DEEZ NUTZ.

In conclusion, I'd like to say that I'm truly sorry we had such trouble arranging to meet up, Ms. Robb.

I realize that journalism depends on good faith and trust between journalists and sources, and I'd hate to see our repeated poor luck inspire unscrupulous or mischievous fellows to waste the time of well-meaning journalists like yourself. If journalists had to wonder every time they made an appointment and were required to buy a right-wing hat if this was some sort of trick to embarrass them, it's possible that no journalism would ever get done at all. Is that the kind of world you want to live in? I don't. I'd be worried about all the blood rushing out of my brain from the massive schadenfreude erection I would get.

P.S. Ms. Robb, shall we try once more? I'll be at Famous Ray's pizza in Brooklyn on Tuesday at noon. No, the other one. This time, I swear I'll show up.

P.P.S. Wear the hat.

CASTALIA HOUSE

### Non-Fiction
*Winning the War on Weeds* by John Moody
*Ship of Fools* by C. R. Hallpike
*The Last Closet* by Moira Greyland
*The Nine Laws* by Ivan Throne
*A History of Strategy* by Martin van Creveld
*Compost Everything* by David the Good
*Grow or Die* by David the Good
*Push the Zone* by David the Good
*Free Plants for Everyone* by David the Good

### Fiction
*Turned Earth: a Jack Broccoli Novel* by David the Good
*The Missionaries* by Owen Stanley
*The Promethean* by Owen Stanley
*An Equation of Almost Infinite Complexity* by J. Mulrooney
*Six Expressions of Death* by Mojo Mori
*Loki's Child* by Fenris Wulf
*Hitler in Hell* by Martin van Creveld

### Military Science Fiction
*There Will Be War Volumes I and II* ed. Jerry Pournelle
*Riding the Red Horse Volume 1* ed. Tom Kratman and Vox Day
*Starship Liberator* by David VanDyke and B.V. Larson
*Battleship Indomitable* by David VanDyke and B.V. Larson

### Science Fiction
*CTRL-ALT REVOLT!* by Nick Cole
*Soda Pop Soldier* by Nick Cole
*Pop Kult Warrior* by Nick Cole
*City Beyond Time* by John C. Wright
*Superluminary* by John C. Wright
*Back From the Dead* by Rolf Nelson

### Fantasy
*No Gods Only Daimons* by Kai Wai Cheah
*Iron Chamber of Memory* by John C. Wright
*The Green Knight's Squire* by John C. Wright
*The Dark Avenger's Sidekick* by John C. Wright

9 789527 303580